FIREPROOF

FIRE PROOF

A FIVE-STEP MODEL
**TO TAKE YOUR LAW FIRM
FROM UNPREDICTABLE**
TO WILDLY PROFITABLE

MIKE MORSE
WITH JOHN NACHAZEL

LIONCREST
PUBLISHING

FIREPROOF

A Five-Step Model to Take Your Law Firm
from Unpredictable to Wildly Profitable

ISBN 978-1-5445-0855-9 *Hardcover*
      978-1-5445-0853-5 *Paperback*
      978-1-5445-0854-2 *Ebook*

This book is dedicated to my father, Joel Morse, for teaching me that being a lawyer can be the most rewarding job in the world.

CONTENTS

FOREWORD

I started working with Michael Morse thirteen years ago.

When I met Michael, he was bursting with raw talent and ambition. I feel honored to have worked directly with him and his leadership team as their Entrepreneurial Operating System (EOS) implementer. I taught them how to implement the EOS tools and practices I lay out in my book *Traction*. EOS is a system for helping any entrepreneur run a better business in any industry.

The vital ingredient that makes EOS work in helping entrepreneurs build great companies is that they have to be entrepreneurs first. Michael Morse is a true entrepreneur, as you will see by his story. Michael would have succeeded in any business. Fortunately for you, he chose law. He will show you how to build a successful law firm.

Michael added John Nachazel as his chief operating officer in 2008, and together, they have achieved a level of success rarely seen in business. It was the perfect visionary-integrator combination, which is why I feature them in my book *Rocket Fuel*.

In addition to being a great entrepreneur, Michael is also a marketing genius. His advertising has transformed him into a local celebrity and taken his business and life beyond what he ever imagined was possible.

John is a master of data. He is one of the best I've ever seen at utilizing data to run a business. I have never seen anyone do more impressive work with data than John.

Combining the EOS tools in *Traction*, Michael's marketing genius, and John's data mastery was like throwing gasoline on a fire (no pun intended). The combination was a triple threat, and now, that explosive strategy is available and customizable for your law firm.

If you are a lawyer and you are committed to running your law firm like a wildly successful business, it is imperative that you read *Fireproof*.

Enjoy the journey and stay focused,
Gino Wickman
Creator of EOS and author of *Traction*

PROLOGUE

A STORY OF SELF-RELIANCE

I learned at an early age that if I was going to be happy, I had to rely on myself.

I grew up in suburban metro Detroit. I was just a normal Jewish kid from a middle-class family. My dad was a solo lawyer, doing general law stuff with an emphasis on personal injury. My mom was a retired school librarian and stay-at-home mom. When I was twelve, my parents divorced, and the world my sister and I lived in was shattered.

My dad remarried, but his new wife hated us. She would tell people when they asked her about "Joel's kids" that they were dead to her. Lovely. My mom also remarried, and her new husband was physically abusive. My stepfather was a psychologist who lost his license for sleeping with a patient. As a result, we moved to another town, and I had to start high school without a single friend. This made me a target for some of the school bullies. They threatened me with beatings, but my cunning ability to avoid danger and talk my way out of threatening situations kept me safe. Still, this was not a very happy time in my life.

By the time I was fifteen, my survival skills were razor sharp. I started working—partly to get out of the house but also as a way to protect myself. If I couldn't find comfort, protection, and stability at home, perhaps I could find it through work. So I took a job busing and waiting tables. This kept me busy. It's not like schoolwork and friends were taking up any time. That's one of the good things about working in restaurants. It is usually a bunch of misfits looking for connections and a job. My coworkers in the fifteen-plus restaurants I have worked in have always become my close friends and somehow part of my family. This is a real thing and happens in most jobs of this nature.

I'm not joking when I say that waiting tables taught me everything I needed to know to be a great trial lawyer.

Good evening, folks! My name is Michael, and I'll be your waiter this evening.

I learned how to think on my feet. I learned how to juggle

five tasks at once while keeping a smile on my face and thinking ahead to what I would do next. I learned how to read customers. I learned how to communicate quickly and clearly to chefs, hostesses, and diners. I developed a fantastic memory. I followed certain practices that allowed me to work faster and more efficiently. I figured out what type of table made me the most in tips, and I learned how to encourage the hostess to seat the four businessmen in my section and give the mother with three toddlers to someone else. I loved the pace, the demands, the pressure. I loved doing an excellent job for my customers, and I loved depositing a fat wad of bills from tips in the bank every day.

The more I worked, the bigger that wad got.

I told myself that the more money I had, the more protected I would be from bullies, stepparents, and whoever else wanted to mess with me. Because of these mistaken beliefs, there were periods when I would work three different restaurant jobs at a time. I would keep the uniforms in my trunk for quick changes. There were many days where I would go from school to a lunch job and then immediately to a different dinner restaurant. Earning money became a game. All those years of waiting tables and finding ways to make more and more. At the end of the night, the manager closing everyone out would always comment that I had the highest in total sales "again." It just came easy to me.

Looking back on it, not only was I developing great lawyer skills, but I was also learning a thing or two about following smart business practices.

In truth, I always had a knack for business. I had a paper route when I was younger, and as a ten-year-old, I used to do odd jobs around my uncle's drugstore. His kids hated going to work with my uncle, but I loved it. I worked the counters with the cashier, and I would interact with the customers and arrange items in a way that made the products more appealing and easier to purchase. I ran the cash register like a pro, and I often made suggestions on ways my uncle could improve customer service. I even made money at school. For instance, Bubblicious bubble gum was all the rage back then, so I would purchase boxes of the stuff and sell it for a profit out of my locker. I couldn't help myself.

RESILIENCE

This book is about business principles—and how I applied cutting-edge business practices to a traditional law firm and experienced astonishing results.

But the backstory for this book is about perseverance. It's about overcoming setbacks. I was knocked down many times in my early career, and as devastating as some of those blows were, I always picked myself up, dusted myself off, and forged ahead.

After high school, I went to college at the University of Arizona in Tucson—about as far from Detroit as you can get and still be in the continental United States. The plan was to get my bachelor's degree and then my law degree so I could work with my dad in his firm.

My father, Joel Samuel Morse, was the kindest and most loving father anyone could want. He was funny and affectionate, and he loved life and loved being a lawyer. His clients loved him. He also had a great rapport with fellow attorneys and judges. My dad was a solo practitioner, and though he wanted me to work for a large law firm, my goal was to be his partner. He made law fun. Why wouldn't I want to work with him?

In 1989, I enrolled in the University of Detroit Law School, which I chose so I could be close to my dad. After class, I would go to my father's law office to study. My dad would drop in while I studied, and we'd read cases together. He was very patient and explained things to me in a way I understood. Although I was a mediocre high school student and college student, I was an outstanding law school student. I started law school thinking everyone was smarter than me. I finished among the top ten students in my class.

In May 1990, I was taking my first-year final exams. They were brutal. I remember talking with my dad from a payphone in the law school lobby after one of the exams. He was in Mexico giving a lecture at a bar association conference, and he wanted to know how the exams were going. He was encouraging. We talked about what I was planning to do that summer. He had helped me get a job with the largest personal injury firm in Michigan at the time. He wanted me to learn from "real" lawyers who knew more than him. He thought that would give me a broader perspective. He was right, and I would give my daughters the same advice today.

After I said goodbye to my dad from the law school lobby, I drove to my mother's house for a long, hard weekend of studying for my remaining finals.

My mother greeted me at the garage door. She looked pale.

"It's your father," she said. "He's had a massive heart attack in Mexico. He's dead, Michael."

He was only forty-nine. I was devastated.

I felt lost and numb. My best friend and the only reason I was in law school had just died. I was twenty-two and had no clue what to do. I wanted to drop out of school. I wanted to run away. But I knew my dad would want me to finish and take over his legacy of helping people.

So that's what I did.

LEARNING THE ROPES

I graduated cum laude from law school and was voted most likely to succeed and most likely to make the most money by my classmates. I took a job with my dad's best friend and former law clerk and spent the next few years learning the nuts and bolts of being a lawyer. I learned how to take depositions. I learned how to try cases. I learned how to bring in cases. I learned how to market myself, and I learned how to win.

And I learned how to make money. By the mid-1990s, I was making more than six figures a year and driving a shiny red BMW 325xi. I got married, and my wife and I started planning to have children.

Then, without warning and for no clear reason, my dad's best friend fired me. I remember it well because I was fired on my dad's birthday—September 21, 1995. He would have been fifty-five. But instead of spending time mourning him, I had to figure out how to rebuild my career.

I was fired on a Friday, and by Monday, I had my own office. I shared a receptionist and worked at a rented desk. I had no cases, clients, or steady lead generators. I had no real money to advertise.

At the time, most personal injury lawyers in Detroit advertised in the Yellow Pages. There were hundreds of full-page ads for attorneys, and those ad spaces cost thousands of dollars a month. They were not arranged alphabetically but sold on a first-come, first-served basis. Even if I could afford one of those full-page ads, I would be at the back of the book behind all the other attorneys.

But I noticed that there were small display ads in front of those impressive full-page ads. These smaller ads only cost hundreds of dollars and were arranged alphabetically. Hmm. I started a small business called An Attorney Who Cares About You and bought an ad to run in front of everyone else.

It worked. The calls started coming in.

I also knocked on the doors of other law firms, introducing myself and offering to take the cases and trials the other lawyers didn't want. It didn't matter to me how small the case was. I took dog-bite cases, slip-and-fall cases—you name it. But I worked them like they were multimillion-dollar cases, calling insurance adjusters every day to get more for my clients. I wanted to maximize these settlements so that the other attorneys would send me more cases.

I developed a reputation for saying no to low-ball settlement offers and taking insurance companies to trial and winning. I could turn a rejected case into thousands of dollars in settlements and referral fees, and in time, other lawyers started calling *me* to find out how I managed to get so much money from these weak cases.

I worked out deals with these other firms: my fee was split fifty-fifty, but the firms would pay all the costs on the files. It was a win-win. I would get free trial practice at no cost to me, whether I won or not. I learned to keep saying no to the insurance companies and pushing them toward trial. When I did this, they would usually offer more money. If they didn't, I still came out ahead because I had a knack for trying cases. I learned that when you say no more and try more cases, you do better. I follow this philosophy today.

MY BIG BREAK

Around this time, I grew close to my father-in-law, the late Steve Radom. Steve plays a major role in this book because he became a mentor and introduced me to so many of the business principles we discuss in the coming pages. Steve was a brilliant businessman and had helped a number of millionaires in Detroit build their wealth.

Steve introduced me to an attorney we'll call Sid. Sid was the premier personal injury attorney in Detroit. He spent over $10 million a year on advertising, and he made much of his money by referring out his cases to other attorneys in town. Sid agreed to get on a phone call with me.

I was extremely nervous. Sid was the big gorilla in town, an advertising and marketing god. Sid had been advertising his law firm on television since the early 1980s. He held tremendous sway in the legal community. He could make or break a person's career.

We made small talk. Sid remembered my dad and said some nice things about him. Then he asked, "What kind of cases are you interested in?"

"Preferably auto cases," I said, "but I'll take anything."

"Slip and fall?"

"I love those cases," I lied.

"Great," he said. "I'll put you on our list." He said I'd pay him 40 percent of the total fees. I knew that one-third was the normal rate, but I accepted the requirement anyway. I wanted to get my phone ringing.

When we hung up, I almost fell out of my chair in excitement. Within days, I was receiving referrals from Sid's office. I thought it was raining gold. When a fax came in from Sid, I dropped everything and called the client. I wanted to make sure no one referred to me by Sid or anyone else would ever have any reason to complain about the service they received from me. I took as much time as was needed on the phone with these clients, and I often visited them at their homes to discuss their case face-to-face. It wasn't easy getting on Sid's referral list, and I wasn't going to blow this opportunity.

One of the early clients was a woman who had tripped in a local grocery store. I raced over to her house to meet her. She had a terrible, swollen bruise over her eye from the accident, so I took pictures and had them blown up. I wrote up a quick demand package for the insurance company. The insurance company wanted to meet my client, but I said she was elderly and not doing well. The case was probably only worth $2,500, but I got $25,000.

When I sent Sid his check, he immediately called. How did you manage to get this? He was impressed.

He started sending me dozens of cases a week, and some weeks I signed up as many as thirty or forty people. Other types of cases started coming in as well, including the lucrative auto accident cases. Sid would keep the slam-dunk cases, refer the next-best set of cases to his longtime referral partners, and send me the undesirable ones—the ones where the client had a little soreness or a cut somewhere.

I didn't care! These were living and breathing clients who needed me and wanted my help! I made sure they understood everything, and I worked hard to get them fully compensated. I gave them the best customer service experience they had ever had. These were the smaller cases that most firms wouldn't even touch, but I was fully committed to them.

This went on for the next twelve years as my practice grew and the cases got bigger and better. I figured out ways to get the best settlements for these smaller cases. I said no to the insurance companies. I went to trial.

It worked.

I won—again and again.

PUTTING OUT FIRES

Although my practice grew larger than I ever dreamed, it was something of a house of cards. It was profitable, growing, respected, and well run, but it was also vulnerable. The firm made millions every year, but I could not shake the feeling that it could all fall at any moment.

What's more, I couldn't stop feeling like no matter how hard I worked, I could never reach solid ground. The earth often felt like it was crumbling under my feet, even as I was winning cases. I was getting cases referred to me by several different sources, but I knew that flow could stop without a moment's notice. Maybe it was because of the difficulties I had experienced to date: divorce, death of a parent, being fired from a job or getting bullied. I was living with the overwhelming question hanging over my head: when would the other shoe drop?

I don't feel that way today. With the help of my mentors—starting with my dad and continuing with my father-in-law, my right-hand man John Nachazel, and my brilliant business coach Gino Wickman—I learned how to approach the practice of law differently. All of the traumas I've faced personally and professionally and all the long, hard years of chasing cases in an extremely competitive market led me to reinvent myself and dramatically redefine how to run a law firm successfully. Out of painful things came wonderful things. We have created a system unlike any ever used in a law practice. It's a system based on sound business principles that we have refined for law in such a way that it works no matter how big your office is.

Now John and I want to share with you exactly how we did it. We're going to lay it all out for you and encourage you to adopt our methods so you can enjoy the same success and peace of mind we enjoy. We're also hoping it gives you the courage to overcome your travails and the uncertainties you face in your law practice. These are the tools you need to free yourself from all that.

The first step is to understand that you can't let professional setbacks define you. You have to use them to get better. You have to see them as opportunities.

What follows is the book I wish I had read back in the early '90s when I was first getting out of law school. We're going to talk about all the things they didn't teach you in law school. We're going to use a lot of terms most lawyers aren't familiar with, terms like *annual plans, rocks, accountability,* and *metrics.* We'll explain the value of numbers, the importance of knowing your why and core values, and how to market your firm so you never have to worry again about where your next case is coming from.

You'll learn how to delegate. Most lawyers aren't good at delegating because they think no one can do the work better than they can. That's how I thought. It turned out that there were other people in my office who were better on the phone than me, better at dealing with clients than me, or better at writing appeals. There were people who actually *liked* doing some of the things I hated doing. I learned to delegate to these talented people, and it's freed me up to focus on my business and make it stronger.

The results have been staggering, and nowhere have those changes been more noticeable than in my personal life. I have time for my kids now. I have time to travel and read. I work *on* my business as much as *in* my business.

Many lawyers in Detroit would say that I'm more of a businessman than a trial lawyer. This doesn't bother me. I'm still a trial lawyer—I train the attorneys in my office, I take the cases that are important to me, and I work very hard to sustain my law practice. I make sure every client who walks through our doors gets the same quality representation that I would give them myself. I'm proud of my law practice, and I'm proud of the lawyers I work with.

And some of these competitors who try and throw shade my way are just purely jealous. Some had law firms handed to them on a silver platter only to allow those firms to stagnate with little or no growth. What we built is unique in the legal world. The more we meet with law firms from around the country, the more we realize how much better our methods are.

I'm equally proud of the business side of my work, and if people want to characterize me as a businessman, I'll wear that hat with pride. As you'll see when you read on, I adopted my business practices out of necessity. I was struggling to manage the firm I'd built, but the business concepts I incorporated not only saved my firm and my employees, but they also enriched my life in unimaginable ways.

Although I'm writing this book in the first person—me to you—I want you to know that my chief operating officer, John, has been my partner in writing this book every step of the way. John and I have worked together to make our process reliable, easy, and scalable. We did it for ourselves. We did it for consistency. We did it for profitability. We did it because it made sense.

Now we want to share our secrets with you. Don't be intimidated by the idea of being entrepreneurial with your law practice. The beauty of our system is that you can make it as simple or as complex as you want. Start small and grow. Or dive in headfirst and start swimming. Either way, if you embrace these ideas, your life will change for the better.

Are you ready? Good. Let's get started.

INTRODUCTION

SMOKE IN THE AIR

The phone went off at three in the morning and roused me from a deep sleep. I normally silence my phone at night, but for some reason, this call came through. I sat up in bed and listened intently to the urgent voice at the other end.

I knew it was bad.

I jumped into the car and headed out. It was a hot July night, and I sped down the highway with the windows open. The road was empty, the way it is in movies after an apocalypse. Nothing seemed real to me, but this wasn't a dream. It wasn't a movie.

About a mile from my exit, I could smell the smoke in the

air. As I got close, I could see the night sky lit up with flashing emergency lights. Sirens were wailing. As I sped down the street to my law office, I could see the fire trucks and the firemen racing around the parking lot, shouting and pointing and carrying equipment and running back and forth. Hoses snaked across the asphalt, and a bitter, black cloud hung in the air, shrouding the light from streetlamps.

Then I saw the flames.

They engulfed my building.

Laurie, my secretary, found me and we embraced, crying. The full impact started to wash over me, making it difficult to catch my breath.

Our staff would have nowhere to work.

Our files. Our cases. Our clients. It seemed our legal practice would be lost. All of it.

How would we recover from this? Could we ever recover?

THE SECOND ALARM

Fast forward three years.

At this time, Sid, the prominent Detroit attorney I mentioned in the prologue, sent my firm 70 percent of our personal injury cases. I built my firm on Sid's referrals. We treated his cases like gold, giving them nothing but the highest level of service and attention. We paid him more than $4 million a year in referral fees.

Then one day in 2011, he called and said we needed to talk. Today.

"I'll come to you," I said.

"No," he replied. "I'll come to you."

He'd never been to our offices before. What was going on?

I knew another fire was brewing.

He arrived a short time later. My receptionist walked him down to my office. He came in, shut the door, and sat on my couch. There was no small talk.

"We're changing direction," he said, his cold gaze leveled on me. "I won't be sending you any more cases."

I was stunned. I don't remember what I said, but I do remember my visitor had little else to say by way of explanation. He rose from the couch and walked out, leaving me to calculate the damage. Seventy percent of our business had just disappeared in an instant. What was I going to do? Did I need to start laying people off? Today?

FIREPROOF

These two devastating blows—the fire in 2008 and being fired by Sid in 2011—threatened to destroy all I had built up over the years since I'd gone into private practice in 1995.

At the time of the fire, I was managing a firm of about two dozen attorneys, paralegals, and administrative personnel. We were on a tremendous trajectory. My firm had grown each year, and after several years of managing every aspect of the operation myself, I'd added some structure and business practices to our office. Those changes freed me to focus on cultivating new business and training our staff to provide the same level of service I had always delivered.

These twin tragedies threatened everything. But like all fires, they also cleared the way for something new.

They provided an impetus to change how we ran our law firm and how we conducted business. How we hired and fired. How we measured our success. How we handled cases and served our clients. The fires brought me new people, new strategies, and wild success.

It's the kind of success that any lawyer—even someone with

a small firm—can replicate if they follow the practices we developed in the wake of these calamities. We found a way to fireproof our law office.

Since that fire destroyed our office, my firm has grown by about 25 percent a year. We've gone from an office of about twenty-five people and $17 million in total settlements and verdicts to an office of 150 employees, including fifty attorneys, and more than $160 million in settlements and verdicts in 2018. We're now the largest personal injury firm in the state of Michigan and have been for several years.

Since Sid fired us, we have become one of the best-known law firms in the state, with an $8 million annual advertising budget that has allowed us to shape and hone our image and ensure that the people who need us can find us. The advertising we launched after Sid fired us has made me a household name in Michigan and has given me the freedom to focus exclusively on what I love to do and what I'm good at.

Ironically, after Sid cut us off, we went on to be his largest competitor in our Designated Marketing Area (DMA). I'm not sure he thought of this or wondered if I had the audacity to go head-to-head with him, but that's what I did, and it's paid off handsomely for my firm and me.

I also enjoyed my freedom after parting company with Sid.

I was free from relying on disloyal people who didn't care about me or my firm. I was free from being dependent on anyone else and was able to make and choose my destiny. It took this firing for me to realize I needed and wanted my autonomy. I am not sure I would have ever made the leap had he not pushed me into it. I am so grateful he did.

Unlike most lawyers, we no longer worry about where our next case is coming from. Because we run our office like a business, we set specific annual goals and use practices to ensure we're on pace throughout the year to reach those goals. We track our numbers carefully. I know how many cases are likely to come in each year, how much we'll make from those cases on average, and how long it will take the settlement funds to arrive. I know precisely how many cases we refer out to other lawyers, and I know which of those lawyers is most likely to take a case. In January of each year, John, my chief operating officer, can predict to within one-tenth of 1 percent how much our firm will make that year. He can do the same with my personal income. Many people in our office used to laugh and roll their eyes and place bets when John came up with his projections. But for twelve straight years, he has only gotten more and more accurate, and we have stopped questioning him.

Do I look back with regret and dismay at the adversities that rocked my law firm?

No.

I look back with extreme gratitude.

PRACTICE LAW LIKE A BUSINESS

If you're at all like I was in the years before our fire, you have no idea how to run your law firm like a business. You know how to run it like a law firm.

You don't know how to advertise or market properly for new clients or how to organize your office to ensure it runs efficiently and profitably. You've never had an executive team, and you've never hired a third-party business coach to help you to figure out what you want your law practice to be, how you want it to grow, and what tactics you're going to use to get there.

Why *would* you know how to do any of this?

We're lawyers, after all. We know how to try cases and spot issues. We earned law degrees, not MBAs. We're clueless about things like key performance metrics, CFOs and COOs, and human resource departments. No one taught us how to run an effective meeting, let alone set business goals. Terms like *rocks* and *forecasting* don't mean much to us. We don't collect data, and we wouldn't know how to analyze it anyway.

We're too busy to think about these things, and we're skeptical of anyone who might suggest we should.

That's okay. Skepticism is good. You have to have a healthy dose of skepticism to succeed in law.

So let me throw some numbers at you.

Since my firm began embracing the principles and practices outlined in this book, it has not only increased profit but has also blossomed in many other ways. When you walk into our offices, you think you're entering a workspace in Silicon Valley. We've created work teams for lawyers, and we use market research and data to determine not only when to advertise but also where to run our ads. We've adopted a hiring process that ensures we hire only those who embody our core values, and we use testing to help determine who's a good fit and where they can best help our firm. We pay our people top dollar, and we have an accountability program that ensures they deliver.

As a result, my firm's revenue is thirteen times higher than it was in 2007. My personal income is ten times higher than it was ten years ago, and I work less. I have time to pursue more of my interests while relying on my chief operating officer to ensure that all the trains run on time loaded with happy passengers. I have the time to drive my daughters to school in the morning and make their lunches.

WHAT YOU CAN EXPECT

I know, I know. You think I'm selling you something and you're wondering what's the catch. There's no catch.

My goal with this book is to share the vital principles I've learned in the last fifteen years about running a law office like a business. I've broken our process down into five distinct steps, each detailed in its own chapter. You may think you don't have enough time to adopt some of these practices, but following the principles in this book will give you back your time. You'll have time to focus on doing what you love and cultivating the clients you crave. You will work less and make more.

Here's an overview of what you'll learn:

◊ **Chapter 1: Know Thyself.** What do the best law firms have in common? They have the best people. They have discovered their core values, and they live those values every day. This first step unleashes the growth potential for your firm while giving you a more lucrative and rewarding life.

◊ **Chapter 2: Hiring, Firing, and Paying.** If you're still following traditional hiring and compensation practices, it's time to change. The second step is to learn how to use testing to find the right people and incentives to ensure those great employees continually produce and improve.

🔥 **Chapter 3: The Jumbotron Principle.** How do you know if you're winning when you don't know what the score is? The third step in running your firm like a business is to create a Legal Jumbotron—a simple system that measures key metrics and tells you day to day how much you're making and whether you're ahead or behind your projections.

🔥 **Chapter 4: Run Your Business like You Run Your Biggest Case.** To win your biggest case, you need a carefully executed plan. Your law firm is no different. You need to know who, what, when, where, why, and how. This is step four.

🔥 **Chapter 5: Cherry Garcia Beats Vanilla.** What makes you the person who people want to hire? When I look out at the attorneys who advertise, I see vanilla flavors. When I advertise, I want people to know I'm a Cherry Garcia guy, a flavor that stands out. Step five in our process will help you learn about your local market and help you develop advertising that works.

🔥 **Conclusion: "He Who Represents Himself Has a Fool for a Client."** Abraham Lincoln said this about lawyers, but he could have been talking about any business endeavor. A lawyer who tries to adopt business principles without outside help from a coach will struggle.

PREDICTABLE AND PROFITABLE

I'm not here to regale you with stories about my biggest cases. My law firm has indeed enjoyed crazy success, but my real goal in writing this book is to share with you some simple ideas for running your firm like a business so you can reap the rewards.

I'm not offering you vague or theoretical practices. Instead, these are road-tested strategies that have worked for us and for businesses everywhere. Many of the techniques I'll describe in the coming chapters have been around for years, but it's rare to find them in use at most law practices. We adopted these practices years ago, and since then, we've supercharged them and refined them to work flawlessly for any law firm. I know these practices work because we've seen them work for us year after year.

They'll work for you, too.

Everything in this book is within your grasp. I'll outline the basic steps, give you the essential tools, and explain how to apply them to the practice of law. I've also set up a website (855mikewins.com/fireproof) for you that includes worksheets and best practices for following the principles we describe in this book. There is a ton of useful information there and we're always adding more.

As easy and practical as we'll make it, this process will likely require you to rethink how you approach your law practice. You may want to restructure your office, change your hiring practices, build a better leadership team, and distribute your work differently.

Whether you're a small office of just three people or a growing practice with a dozen people, adopting the principles we describe in this book will make your firm more predictable as well as more profitable. I took action when I had twenty employees, but I should have started sooner.

My advice is to stop making excuses. Read on, and find out how you can change your office, get your life back, and make more money in the process.

Find out how to be fireproof.

CHAPTER 1

KNOW THYSELF

FEELING OVERWHELMED

Twenty years ago, I was making good money, but I was working twelve hours a day. I was so busy practicing law that I had no time for the business side of things. I knew money was coming in, but I didn't know how much money we had in the bank. I was so busy earning money that I had no time to count it.

During this period, my quality of life was declining. My wife and I started having children in 1999, but I never had enough time to spend with my daughters. I was exhausted all the time. I was always running, running, running. In 2005, ten years after starting my practice, I had seven people working for me. By 2007, I had nineteen. In these two years, I nearly tripled the size of my firm while maintaining my own full caseload. I also did all the hiring, training, and onboarding. I decided who sat where and made sure they had computers, secretaries, and supplies. I made all the decisions and signed all the checks. I reviewed the settlement statements and handled all of the trials. I could go on and on, but you get it. I had no real help. The people who worked for me were merely my employees.

I was trying to be a good lawyer and run a great law firm.

And I was dying.

I never let on to my staff how overwhelmed I was, but my father-in-law could see I was struggling. He repeatedly advised me to hire a coach to show me how to run the firm more efficiently. I said I didn't have the money, which was not true, and I said I didn't have the time.

"Make the time, Michael," Steve said. "Make some time now, and you'll have more time for the rest of your life. It's a good investment."

Eventually, I made that investment.

GETTING HELP

I hired a business coach in 2007. Two friends recommended Gino Wickman, a business coach living outside Detroit. Although Gino had never worked with a law firm before, he assured me that the principles are the same regardless of the business.

The first step in the process was an off-site retreat. Gino told me to bring my leadership team.

"I don't have a leadership team," I said.

"Yes, you do," he said. "You may not call them a leadership team, but you have a group of people around you whom you trust and rely on. Bring them."

So I told Laurie, my assistant, Marc, my top lawyer, and Jan, my top paralegal, that we were going to close the office and meet with a business coach. They looked at me like I was crazy. Close the office? We have too much work to do. But I insisted.

The first activity involved going around the table and talking about what we were struggling with. I went last. I laid out my problems and how it was affecting my family and happiness. I had nineteen direct reports, in addition to my own 150 cases. I approved everyone's work, did their evaluations, calculated their bonuses, and generally acted as their guidance counselor. I allowed myself to admit I was overwhelmed.

The table was silent for a few moments. I don't think Jan, Marc, and Laurie were used to me being so vulnerable.

"What if the lawyers all reported to me from now on?" asked Marc. Marc was one of the first lawyers I hired, and he's still with me.

"I'll be in charge of the secretaries," Laurie said.

"Michael, when the paralegals have a question, I'll have them come to me from now on," Jan said.

I was astonished. By the end of the day, my workload was 50 percent lighter. I felt instant relief. It was an emotional meeting. It was also a surprising turn of events. These people didn't have to step up this way—there was no discussion about paying them more for taking on more responsibility. But I'd recruited each of them and had followed my father-in-law's advice to find the best and pay them better than the market rate. They were great people, and now these superstars were rising to the occasion. Of course, I eventually paid them more, but that's not why they stepped up the way they did that day, and that meant everything.

The changes took effect the minute we returned to the office. I was relieved, but I also wondered why I hadn't made these moves earlier.

In retrospect, I can see that I was not equipped to deal with a business of this size alone and without guidance. I just didn't have the business experience to figure it out on my own. But delegating some of my responsibilities was such an easy thing. It brought such profound and long-lasting results that it gave me the confidence to start examining other possible changes. Our structure has evolved since that first meeting, but I often think back to that day and the insights I learned. I don't bite off more than I can chew anymore—ever. I learned my lesson and am not going back.

FINDING OUR CORE STRENGTHS

One of the next things we did was to determine the firm's core values. I guarantee you that few law firms have talked about core values or identified theirs. I was skeptical about the benefits of core values.

But since then, I've learned that core values are crucial to your success. They determine whom you hire, whom you fire, and whom you reward. They dictate how you work and how you grow and how you approach your clients. They are central to everything you do.

Your core values and core purpose—the two faces of your core ideology—define what makes your firm great and what the people who work there believe. Core values are not aspirations, goals, or a vision but a truthful measure of how your firm operates, what it values most, and why your employees love to show up at work every morning. To discover your core values, ask yourself, What qualities does my firm have that make it successful? What is it about my people that convinces clients to seek us out and return to us when they need help?

Somewhere in the answer to those questions are your core values.

WHY CORE VALUES ARE CRUCIAL

I know some of you are probably thinking, "Hey, we're a law firm. We pursue justice for our clients. That's our core value. Isn't that all we need?"

The answer is no.

You need more than that.

According to Verne Harnish, author of *Scaling Up*, well-thought-out and resonant core values are critical to any company's long-term growth. Well-articulated core values attract employees who share those values and allow them to flourish under your roof. They repel those who don't hold the same values. Those people feel out of place and are probably happier working somewhere else. People used to be willing to put up with a work climate that didn't suit them because they needed the job. But professionals these days want something more. They still like big paychecks, but they also want to feel part of something that offers intangible rewards.

Jim Collins and Jerry Porras pioneered the idea of core ideology in 1994 when they released their book *Built to Last: Successful Habits of Visionary Companies*. For six years, Collins and Porras had studied some of the most successful companies in the world and found that those who succeed have well-defined core values and core purpose. That core ideology, they found, doesn't change even as the companies' business strategies and practices adapted to the changing world around them.

Collins and Porras make a distinction between core values, vision, and future growth. Although law firms and companies can focus on scaling up, perhaps even spreading into new areas of business, their core values never change. Your vision for your firm should involve preserving your core principles while you explore future progress and opportunities. The best organizations view their core ideology as their "timeless guiding principles."

HOW TO FIND YOUR CORE VALUES

When you work with a business coach—something I recommend for anyone reading this book—you learn that you never *create* core values; you *discover* them. Core values are not aspirational. They are not what you *wish* you could be; they are what you already *are*. They're authentic. You're passionate about them. Your core ideology is inspiring to you but isn't designed to inspire outsiders.

If your firm is at least five years old, those values are already in place. Your firm already has a personality. It already has habits and inclinations that guide its day-to-day work and decisions. What you need to do is discover what those behaviors and values are and codify them.

To discover your core values, Collins and Porras recommend that you nominate a group of five to seven individuals from your company who are highly competent, have great credibility within the organization, and already seem to be living a set of essential core values. They represent a "slice of the company's genetic code." Most companies put their leader, their founders, and a few of their best executives or employees on the job.

The authors call this team the Mars Group because the team is asked to travel to a new world to re-create the best attributes of their company. This group, the authors say, must "push with relentless honesty to define what values are truly central."

According to Collins and Porras, each value has to pass a critical test:

If the circumstances changed and penalized us for holding this core value, would we still keep it?

If the answer is yes, you just might have a core value. (See the sidebar "Testing Your Core Values" for other questions you must consider.)

Some business coaches don't like using a Mars Group to discover a firm's core values. They say that approach works for multibillion-dollar companies with thousands of employees. Gino, our coach, used a different strategy. He took us through an exercise of getting each of us to think of three people who exemplify our core values. We put their names on the board and then we listed the characteristics that describe those people. From there, we culled and refined the characteristics until we felt we had the perfect set of principles for our firm.

Harnish agrees that many organizations go about finding their core values the wrong way. A common approach is to assign the core values job to your HR department or to survey employees to come up with a list of possibilities. Mistake. A strong set of core values does not emerge from a democratic process. Harnish says this approach typically results in a meaningless "generic Boy Scout list" of values like "integrity" and "honesty."

Instead, you want honest values written in direct, everyday language that your firm actually uses—not vague or sentimental terms.

It's not an easy process, and it takes time. Business author

Patrick Lencioni recommends you discuss core values over a few months, picturing how the values will affect day-to-day work and searching for values you may have initially overlooked. When it comes to core values, it's better to ruminate and refine rather than roll out something quickly and have it just as quickly lose credibility within your firm.

Discovering and embracing your core values is not a benign experience. It's hard work, and it forces you to be authentic. When a colleague violates a core value, you have to be willing to call them out. Likewise, you have to be ready to hear that you could do a better job of living the firm's core values. For example, at Intel, which values constructive confrontation, new employees are trained in the art of debating and challenging their colleagues' ideas without any hard feelings. Not everyone is comfortable in that kind of setting, and people who aren't might want to consider working for a different firm.

TRAPS TO AVOID

Lencioni noted in a *Harvard Business Review* article that many US companies rushed to establish their core values after *Built to Last* came out in 1994. Establishing core values became a fad, and the result was that more than 80 percent of the *Fortune* 100 companies in the US began touting their core values.

TESTING YOUR CORE VALUES

In their book *Built to Last,* Jim Collins and Jerry Porras say the group members developing your organization's core values have to pose a series of questions:

- What core values do I personally bring to work? What values are so fundamental to me that I would maintain them even if I weren't rewarded for doing so?

- Is this a value you would share with your children and advise them to embrace when they become working adults?

- If you win the lottery this afternoon and can immediately retire, would you continue to hold this value?

- Will this value be as crucial a hundred years from now?

- Would you maintain this value even if it posed a competitive disadvantage?

- If you were moving into a new line of work, would this value carry over to the new endeavor?

Unfortunately, Lencioni wrote, those values "too often stand for nothing but a desire to be *au courant* or, worse still, politically correct." Enron's values were "communication, respect, integrity, and excellence"—values they trumpeted right up to the day the company collapsed under the weight of its fraud and corruption.

Lencioni wasn't criticizing companies for establishing core values. He criticized companies that didn't put in the difficult work to discover the right ones.

"Coming up with strong values—and sticking to them— requires real guts," he wrote, noting that some employees will leave a company if they don't believe in the firm's values. Values can also limit your options when it comes to expanding your business. Values only mean something when they are obsessively embraced—brought up incessantly at staff and executive team meetings, written into job evaluations, incorporated into hiring decisions, and emblazoned on posters and coffee mugs around the office.

There are real risks to having insincere or spurious core values. For one thing, your employees will just roll their eyes and whisper, "Whom are they trying to kid? No one here acts that way!" Managers who roll out bland or innocuous value statements run the risk of being perceived as bland or innocuous themselves. Your customers may also weigh in by opting out—and looking for a firm that does what it says it does.

The rewards of a strong core ideology have been proven time and again, however. People who share your values will love you and want to help you succeed. Your employees will love to come to work every day. Clients will recommend you to their friends. Judges, opposing counsel, and even court clerks will rise to your standards.

You win.

ADDITIONAL THINGS TO CONSIDER

Although *Built to Last* was published more than twenty-five years ago, the book itself has stood the test of time. Successful executives still turn to it as a guide for discovering their company's tenets and personality. Here are some key takeaways from that book:

🔥 Companies should not have a laundry list of values. The best ones have three to five core values.

🔥 Your core purpose, the second part of your core ideology, reflects your idealistic reason for doing the work you do. Its primary purpose is to pilot your firm and inspire its employees.

🔥 Look for employees who are predisposed to sharing your values. You can't impose core values on people, although you should remind them what those values are and point out when they don't embrace them.

OUR CORE VALUES

I want to stress that we couldn't have identified our core values without an independent, third-party mentor compelling us to do it. If you sit around with your company leaders and tried to do it yourself, it's not going to work. You need that guidance. You need that impetus. There are lots of business coaches out there and lots of different programs that they use. Still, many business-development models emphasize the importance of identifying the handful of qualities that make your company different and successful.

We spent a long time discussing our core strengths before we settled on six:

- 🔥 **Hardworking:** We give 100 percent on every job. Our work ethic extends beyond a Monday-through-Friday, nine-to-five schedule because we arrive early, stay late, and work weekends when needed.

- 🔥 **Loyal to the firm:** We care about each other. We don't talk behind each other's backs. If you are loyal to the firm, the firm will be loyal to you.

- 🔥 **Great work:** We produce excellent work products. Our work is impeccable, and we produce it on time with no errors or misstatement of law or facts.

- 🔥 **Dedicated to winning:** We do everything in our power to ensure our clients get what they are entitled to. We aggressively and creatively stand up for our clients' rights. If we don't win, we take it personally. It feels like a punch in the gut.

- 🔥 **Outstanding customer service:** Our clients are often hurt, wary, and sometimes destitute, but we make them feel welcomed and important. We are people pleasers—regardless of how bitter or frustrated our clients might be when they walk in the door. We end every phone call with "Do you have any further questions, or is there anything else I can do for you?"

🔥 **Excellent reputation:** People know us as honest and aggressive. We don't steal cases from other firms. Judges, attorneys, and insurance adjusters know that when we tell them something, it's accurate, and we will live up to our promises.

These are the things that make the Mike Morse Law Firm great, but we had never articulated them or written them down before. We had never screened job candidates to see if they had these same values. We had never analyzed our personnel to ensure that our people embraced these values in their daily work.

That's all changed.

Now our six core values are posted on a big sign in our break room, and we talk about them all the time. They are the filter through which we strain our day-to-day decisions. *Is this great work?* If not, scrap it and redo it. *Is this outstanding customer service?* If not, find a way to make it so.

We established our core values in 2007, and they still resonate today. They form the culture of my firm. We know what our culture is, and we actively manage the company to maintain that culture. And we make sure people know what that culture is. Our culture repels people who aren't a cultural fit, and we attract people who share our values. We've created a haven for like-minded people, and this leads to great efficiency, job satisfaction, and consistency.

Establishing our core values was pivotal to our ability to grow. If you want to work at our firm, you must not only know these core values, you must live them. They are not negotiable. I made it clear to the firm in a formal speech what our values were and what our expectations were: we will not allow people to work here if they cannot or do not embrace these values.

Although I was initially skeptical about core values, I enjoyed taking an in-depth, reflective, and therapeutic look at my firm and its values. And I wish I had established them sooner. We waited until we had more than twenty employees to work on our core values, but I should have started the process when I only had five. You don't have to be a big company to decide on your core values. You can do it with three employees. You can do it if you're a solo practitioner. The earlier you know your destination, and who you are and what you stand for, the easier and faster your journey to success will be.

It's worthwhile for any organization—whether it's a law

office or a nonprofit or a multinational corporation—to take the time to reflect on its work habits and culture and formally articulate its own set of core values. Every company is different. It's folly for any organization—a law firm or otherwise—to adopt our values and call it good. To do this right, you have to identify your core values.

Core values are more than a touchy-feely exercise. They are how you get your people aligned around your practices and your ethical and moral codes. "Imagine all twenty of us working together with a common goal and with a common set of values," I told my staff when I introduced our core values. "No one will be able to stop us!"

One last note on this topic. Notice that we did not put in obvious ones, such as "ethical" or "honest." These traits are in our DNA and must be in every lawyer's DNA.

CORE PURPOSE: FINDING YOUR WHY

Many businesspeople, if you ask them what their why is, they'll say things like "make money" or "expand market share" or something along those lines. But our feeling was that we needed something more compelling than that. Of course people want to make money, but that alone is unfulfilling. You need something more than a paycheck. You need a higher purpose. You have to have a compelling reason to get up in the morning and head into work with enthusiasm.

You need to know your why.

In our case, our why is advocating for our clients to make their lives better. The people who come to us often have been hurt or traumatized, and our job is to help them rebuild their lives and become whole again. This is the catalyst that drives our actions and inspires us to embrace our core values and win.

Collins and Porras spent six years studying companies such as Disney, Marriott, 3M, and HP to discern why their stock performed fifteen times better than the overall stock market for decades. One thing all these great companies had was "a deeply-held core purpose."

> [It's] the organization's fundamental reason for being. An effective purpose reflects the importance people attach to the company's work—it taps their idealistic motivations—and gets at the deeper reasons for an organization's existence beyond just making money.

Collins and Porras's findings have been echoed countless times since their book was first published, most notably by Simon Sinek, whose book *Start with Why* asserts that your core purpose must be idealistic and compelling. It tells the world what you believe, not what you make or how you make it. Your core purpose describes what *value* you are bringing to society, not what product or service you are delivering.

Your core purpose is not supposed to be a goal you achieve but something you strive for every day. Your core purpose also embraces the quality of what makes your business special and successful. For example, we pursue our core purpose (of helping injured people) through personal injury legal actions. We do not allow ourselves to be distracted by opportunities beyond our niche and start taking on cases—such as divorce or bankruptcy—outside our specialty. We believe the adage that if you chase two rabbits, both get away. Our core purpose keeps us focused, motivated, and incredibly successful.

In his book *The Infinite Game*, Sinek refers to core purpose as a "just cause." He says your just cause must stand for something, help others, and be idealistic—presenting a lofty, noble, and inspiring vision. Your just cause also must be capable of withstanding economic or political disruption and be open to others who want to join your crusade.

Like core values, your core purpose is easier to find when you have an independent third-party advisor, such as a business coach, working with you. One way to get close to your core purpose is to use the Five Whys exercise, a root-cause analysis method used by Toyota to perfect its lean manufacturing and near-zero-error production system.

Here's how it works: you start with a simple description of your work and then ask *Why is that important?* until you drill down to your root cause. In our case, we are a personal injury law firm.

Why is that important?

We help people get compensated for their injuries.

Why is that important?

We help individuals who don't have the knowledge, time, and money to fight insurance companies.

Why is that important?

We help struggling people receive just compensation for their suffering.

As you drill down, you can see how your core purpose becomes more idealistic and inspiring. Your just cause was there all along, but perhaps you didn't think of it this way before. Now you do, and your work becomes more purposeful and vital now.

FINDING THE VISIONARY

During the time we worked on our core values and core purpose, our business coach introduced me to two significant business ideas:

🔥 The visionary and the integrator.

🔥 Delegate and elevate.

I'd never heard of the terms *visionary* and *integrator* before. It was a concept Gino developed, and he and coauthor Mark C. Winters wrote about it in their book *Rocket Fuel*.

Visionaries, Gino taught us, had powerful imaginations. They have clear mental images of how things should look. They love to create and learn and generate new ideas. They're entrepreneurial, and they're fantastic with valuable clients. In most companies, the CEO is the visionary.

As I read about the characteristics of a visionary, I realized that I had those characteristics myself.

But I also learned that an integrator is just as vital to a business as a visionary. Integrators unite all the functions of a business. They conduct the orchestra. They create the focus of a company, develop ways to hold people accountable and make sure everyone is rowing in the same direction. The integrator is the visionary's number-two person.

The visionary prefers to scan the thick report and wants only the highlights. The integrator reads the whole thing, including all the footnotes and appendices. The visionary is the wow, and the integrator is the how.

History is full of visionaries and integrators who do amazing things together. Ray Kroc dreamed of being able to buy the same burger for the same price at any one of a million McDonald's restaurants across the country. It was a grand vision. But his integrator, Fred Turner, was the guy who dove into the minutiae and made it happen. Henry Ford invented the automobile assembly line, but James Couzens was the general manager who built the company into the behemoth it became. Walt Disney was a dreamer and his brother Roy ran the business side of things. After Walt died, Roy came out of retirement to oversee the construction of Walt Disney World.

As I read about the characteristics of an integrator, I knew right away that it wasn't me. I didn't know anyone who was an integrator.

Besides, I thought, what can an integrator do at a *law firm*? We're not an amusement park or a fast-food restaurant. There isn't much call for building rides or installing french fry vats in a law firm. I told our coach this.

"If you want to scale and grow," Gino said, "you need one."

DELEGATE AND ELEVATE

Gino handed me a blank sheet of paper. He told me to write down over the course of the next week everything I loved about running a law firm and was great at, everything I like to do and am good at, everything I don't like to do but I'm still good at, and everything I hate to do and that I'm not good at.

He called it a "delegate and elevate" exercise. I wasn't sure what he meant by that, but over the next several days, I followed his directions and made notes on the sheet.

The next week, when I handed him the sheet back, he took out a red pen and circled the column of things I loved to do and am great at.

"Here's your sweet spot," he said. "If you want to grow your company and you want to stop feeling overwhelmed, these are the only things I want you to work towards doing and nothing else."

"Who is going to do these eighty-seven other things?" I asked.

"You have to delegate those things," he said.

"To whom?"

"Your integrator," he said. "Now go out and find one."

This was in 2008. I knew Gino was right, but I was still hesitating. A few weeks later, I got that 3:00 a.m. call from the fire department and drove across town to watch my building burn.

I was going to need some help. I had no choice but to act on my need for an integrator.

ENTER OUR NEW COO

Although I agreed with the *idea* of an integrator, I was skeptical about hiring one for the firm.

For one thing, what do you call this person? Terms like *chief operating officer*, *director of operations*, and *general manager* were thrown around, but all these terms were foreign to me. Law firms don't have positions like that. They might have an office manager or a managing partner, but I couldn't think of one law firm that had a chief operating officer.

On top of that, there was the question of salary. My research showed that COOs make more than six figures. That sounded crazy to me.

"If you get the right person and they do a good job, they'll pay for themselves," Steve, my father-in-law, told me. "It'll be worth it. And if the person works out, they could be with you for a long time."

FREE TO FOCUS: THE DELEGATE-
AND-ELEVATE EXERCISE

A lawyer just starting usually has to be a jack-of-all-trades. You do all the writing, research, phone calls, court appearances, trials, billing, and bookkeeping. You have to request the right documents, read through all the medical records, interview doctors, meet with clients, provide excellent customer service, and on and on. You have to remember to buy malpractice insurance, read up on the new laws, cultivate referral sources, and attend seminars.

It's rare to find an attorney who is good at all of those things. They are good at some things, less good at others, and terrible at some aspects of the job. As a result, they are inevitably going to spend time doing tasks that they don't enjoy and aren't good at, and in most cases, those are tasks that someone getting paid less can do for you. The last thing you want is a highly paid attorney doing menial tasks. That's not financially smart.

That's why I have everyone on my executive team do the delegate-and-elevate exercise. I give them a blank sheet of paper, and on the right-hand side they write down all the things about their job that they don't like to do and aren't good at, and on the left-hand side they write down all the things they love to do and are good at.

The goal is to get everybody doing what they love doing and are good at. If you can get people in their sweet spot, they blossom and start having a big impact on the growth and profitability of your firm.

It may take a while to get there. In some cases, it can take years. But if you do the delegate-and-elevate exercise, you establish a goal, and you can work toward achieving it.

It took me several years to whittle away the stuff I was doing that I didn't love to do and wasn't great at, but today I can say that I am in my sweet spot. I'm doing the stuff I love and do well, and my other work goes to people who enjoy that sort of thing and can do it better than me, such as firing. John took that over. I hated to fire people, and poor performers sometimes remained on the job because I didn't like to fire people.

Done well, the delegate-and-elevate exercise frees you to focus on the work that brings your firm the highest return. You learn what your folks' native genius is, and then you get to maximize that inherent ability.

For example, we have one attorney in our office who is great at working up a case, but he doesn't like doing trials. He's not particularly good in a courtroom. But we have another attorney in the office who is great at trials and not as great at working up a case. So we let each one of them do the part they love and are great at, push them together, and the results are extraordinary. Together, their results are exponentially higher than if they were working separately.

When you know your employees' strengths and weaknesses, you can purposely hire people who complement them. We don't spend much time trying to strengthen their weaknesses, but we do spend time discerning their superpowers so we can maximize our return from those abilities.

Patty in our office doesn't have a docket. She loves to settle cases and is great at it, so she invests all her time settling cases for my other lawyers.

In the end, we want to ensure that whoever is doing something for the client is incredible at that aspect of the case and loves working on it.

Integrators don't grow on trees, but one individual quickly rose to the top of our list of candidates. His name was John Nachazel, and at the time we found him, he had been a manager and leader in the auto industry.

Since this was such an essential hire, we pulled out all the tools we had learned to ensure we'd found the right person.

John took the personality tests I'd been using for several years—the ones I'd learned about from Steve. John took the same cognitive skills test they use in the NFL to evaluate players. We probed him about his core values and work ethic. The people who would report directly to John interviewed him. We asked him to read a couple of business books and dug into how he would go about implementing and improving the processes we had adopted.

I told him about myself—my background, my aspirations, my work habits. The good things as well as the bad stuff. I needed to know that he would be able to deal with me and all my foibles.

I was looking for someone to turn my weaknesses into strengths. I had dreams, and I needed someone to help me realize them. I already knew I was a visionary, so I didn't need another one. I needed someone who wanted to get their hands dirty, liked order and accountability, and wanted to dig deep into the numbers. It would also help if he had a sense of humor and the confidence to lead a growing team of crack legal minds.

It was a tall order, but John fit the bill.

Most law firms don't allow employees to interview their future supervisor, but I had my established executive team interview and meet John. I had to make sure they got along with him and respected him, particularly since he isn't an attorney. If they endorsed him, that would give them a stake in John's success. If they'd had a say in his hiring, they would work harder to get along with him and make him successful.

Everybody loved him.

The guy who administered our testing said he'd be an ideal fit. By all measurements—demeanor, intelligence, experience, personality—he was perfect. But would he take the job? I needed someone content with being number two. Would this be enough for him?

John had never considered working for a law firm, but he liked the idea of going from the huge ocean of the auto industry to the small pond of a personal injury law firm. With us, he could have more autonomy. He could have more impact. He liked the idea of working with people devoted to helping others have better lives.

While we evaluated John, he evaluated us. He understood the benefits of our new business practices, but he also knew that if I wasn't committed to following those practices that this new approach would fail. He knew that having complete buy-in at the top was critical to the success of this approach. If I was not willing to take that all-in leap of faith, then John knew the plan would fail.

I convinced him that I was committed. What's more, John was comfortable being my number-two person. He agreed he was best suited to be the integrator to my visionary.

You're hired!

John shared an office with me those first few months—not because we were short on space but because I wanted him to understand what I stood for. I wanted him to see how I handled things. This was my baby. My family. In short order, I would be handing over the day-to-day operations to him, so I wanted him to watch me closely. To listen to me. I wasn't turning over the ship to just a manager. This manager had to know my heart. How I thought. How I analyzed issues and problems and dealt with people. He had to understand I was fiercely loyal to anyone who showed loyalty to me.

He listened in on every conversation and sat in on every meeting I had. I'd give him a preview and a recap after every meeting, and in this way, he learned how I liked to operate and what our office was like. I wanted John to see how I lead. It was critical for me, for our culture, that John carried on my traditions and my compassion for the firm.

FINDING JOHN NACHAZEL

Hiring our COO was part science and part serendipity.

Jerry Spencer, the expert who did our employee testing, met with me and learned what type of person I was looking for. I showed him the long list of duties I wanted to give to our new COO. I needed someone who wasn't afraid to ruffle feathers and knew how to instill some structure, discipline, and accountability. I needed someone who understood numbers and how to use them to make smart business decisions. I needed someone who knew what a core value was and embraced the same core values that I had. We weren't advertising for someone, but we were actively networking, so I told Jerry to be on the lookout for a good candidate.

As it turned out, a good candidate lived two doors down from Jerry. His name was John Nachazel.

Jerry knew John's experience was working in the auto industry, but during a backyard conversation, Jerry learned John was interested in doing something different. John wanted a job where he could have more impact and do a wider variety of things.

"What other kind of job would interest you?" Jerry asked.

"I'd like to run a medium-sized business," John said.

"Are you kidding?" Jerry asked.

"No, I'm serious," John said.

"Well, I just met with Michael Morse and he needs you. You are exactly what he's looking for."

Later, after we offered him the job, John stopped by to talk to Jerry again.

"What do you think?" John asked his neighbor. "Should I go for it?"

> "John," Jerry said, "this feels like it was meant to be. Michael described his ideal candidate in the morning, and I ran into his ideal candidate a few hours later. And he's my neighbor. The world doesn't normally work that way. When that happens, you can't overthink it. You just have to go for it."
>
> So John took my offer. And twelve years later, it still feels like it was meant to be.

It was 100 percent my firm. I had no partners. And it was beyond strange to bring someone in from the outside to run it. Especially a nonlawyer!

John joined the firm a couple of months after the fire. He immediately took over managing the reconstruction of our old office and working with the insurance company to settle our loss-of-business claim. John handled those jobs in short order and then dug in on the eighty-seven other things on my list. We spent much time together and collaborated on many things, but very quickly John took on the work that I couldn't get to, didn't want to have, wasn't good at, and didn't like to do.

EASING INTO THE COCKPIT

Gradually, almost imperceptibly, John took over the day-to-day management of the firm. He blended into what we had initiated. He started collecting data, and our forecasts and business decisions soon became more accurate, timely, and consistent.

He took the numbers from wildly mediocre to far more than useful.

He made them essential.

John reported to me, but everyone else reported to John. This was a little awkward at first, particularly for me, but in time, the arrangement began to operate smoothly.

John remained behind the scenes. My name remained on the door. It was my firm. Clients still asked for me, and judges, defense attorneys, and everyone else who interacted with our firm did not meet John or work with him. John ran the business of the firm but had nothing to do with running the cases. To this day, after twelve years, he has rarely interacted with a client. He doesn't need to understand the law or the types of cases we handle. He *does* need to know which cases are our most profitable. How to get those cases. Which lawyers in the firm get the most money out of those cases, and things like that. The business behind the case.

This sounds unnatural to many of you. It is rare to have a chief operating officer at a law firm. It's rare to have numbers, teams, and core values. Lawyers don't talk about visionaries and integrators.

But if you want to scale your business, these techniques are essential. I hired John when we had about twenty-five employees, but I wish I had hired him when the firm was smaller because this was the only way to free me up to live in my sweet spot. It was the only way I could get time to focus on new clients and our business relationships. These techniques allow me to pursue new marketing ideas, inspire our employees, and work on our most significant cases. I'm free to shoot commercials and do volunteer work in the community—all of which help the firm, help the community, and help me.

When you look at the growth trajectory of my firm, it becomes clear that I was holding the firm back when I insisted on managing everything. I couldn't do what I thought I should be doing, and our growth was limited as a result. When I uncapped the firm and focused on what I was good at and loved to do, we flourished.

Our firm is not just highly profitable. It's also a great place to work. I'm not just saying that; we consistently win best-place-to-work awards by objective measures. We hire the best and pay well, so our top-notch employees aren't required to sacrifice their productivity to prop up weaker employees. Everyone in the office is highly skilled.

Our business coach was so impressed with what we accomplished that he mentioned John and me in his book *Rocket Fuel.*

"Michael is a pure Visionary in every sense," Gino wrote. "He is the face of the company, a true celebrity in the marketplace, an incredible idea guy, amazing with the culture of the company and at inspiring the troops.

"John couldn't be more different. He prefers to remain behind the scenes. He's great at executing Michael's ideas. He loves numbers—forecasting, budgeting, and financial predictions—having dialed in every number in the firm as a science. John is truly the glue that holds the law firm together.

"Michael and John are polar opposites. John's responsibilities and passions are to analyze the data, identify, and explain key revenue and cost drivers, manage people to help problem solve, drive continuous improvement, balance the workload, teach managers how to manage by the numbers, and free up the Visionary to stay in his sweet spot.

"Michael appreciates the need for these responsibilities in his organization, but he's thrilled that he does not have to do them."

Keep in mind that these ideas and approaches can be scaled down. You don't have to have forty attorneys working for you for this to make sense. We started when we had twenty employees, but all of this would have worked at a smaller firm.

SUMMARY

Knowing yourself means knowing your strengths and weaknesses, both as an individual and as a law firm. Knowing your firm's core purpose and core values is a key step in sustaining and growing your practice. It helps you hire the right people, and it helps you ensure everyone in the boat is rowing in the same direction.

Another critical step is identifying your sweet spot—the work you love to do and do extremely well. This is crucial for everyone in your office. When you know everyone's strengths and weaknesses, you can delegate the jobs some hate and aren't good at to people who love that kind of work and can do it much better. When we started doing that, staff productivity went through the roof, and people enjoyed their work more.

Having a strong visionary and strong integrator is also crucial to your firm, but it's only an initial step. The next step involves adopting practices to ensure you hire the best people, pay them according to their abilities, and create an office environment they can thrive in. Read on to learn more.

CHAPTER 2

HIRING, FIRING, AND PAYING

TRADITIONAL HIRING PRACTICES DON'T WORK

The standard hiring process of reading résumés, conducting face-to-face interviews, and checking references is flawed. It's complete guesswork. Candidates fictionalize their résumés, set up shills to serve as references, and schmooze their way through the interview process. You can find any number of studies that show how companies still using traditional hiring practices fail to find the best candidate about 75 percent of the time.

I think references are a complete waste of time. What candidate is going to give you the name of someone who won't give a glowing recommendation? This is why I don't ask for them, and I don't call references if they're given to me. This doesn't mean if the candidate worked for someone I knew or we had mutual friends, I wouldn't call and ask; I would.

If anyone were to trust the interview process, it would be me. I consider myself a great judge of people. I can get them to talk, and I usually can quickly tell if they are nervous, relaxed, angry, or pleased. This comes from my days as a waiter when I prided myself on being able to assess a table and instinctively know what kind of customer I was dealing with. I can read people.

But I don't find the interview process a particularly useful way to learn about someone. People can exaggerate their accomplishments, take credit when it should go to someone else, and pretend to have skills they don't. In other words, candidates can bullshit their way through an interview, bullshit their way into a job, and two months later leave you standing knee-deep in their accumulated bullshit.

I have been fooled by a great interview. In one case, I was blown away by a job candidate during the interview process and hired her without reservation.

Within a couple of months, this person was a major disappointment. She regularly showed up late and left early. Her work product was subpar. She did not live up to any of our values as a firm. We spent weeks training her and working with her but eventually had to let her go. Unfortunately, I overlooked her subpar testing because she was great in the interview.

We learned a vital lesson. Today, a big part of our process at Mike Morse Law Firm is discerning and utilizing each employee's inherent strengths. No two people are alike, so we use a variety of methods to determine which job applicants embrace our core values and have the abilities we need. We only hire when we're convinced applicants have skills that meet our needs and complement the skills of the people already on staff.

HIRE THE BEST FIT

Running your law firm like a business requires smart hiring practices. Again, I learned this from my father-in-law, Steve Radom, during one of our lunches.

This was around 1999, and Steve knew I was running around like a chicken with his head cut off. I was a solo practitioner at the time, and I was staggering from one case to the next, doing all my own writing and scheduling and taking calls. It was clear that I desperately needed a great assistant.

"What kind of person do you want for the job?" Steve asked.

"I don't know. A secretary. Someone who's worked in a law firm before."

He sighed. He did that a lot when he was trying to teach me about business.

"OK, so write down the ten things you want your secretary to be great at," he said.

"I will," I said.

"No," he said. "I mean right now. Write them down."

Now it was my turn to sigh. This felt like some kind of exercise, and I hate doing exercises. When I'm reading a book and the author tells you to put the book down and perform some sort of activity, I skip that section and continue reading. But Steve was my father-in-law, and I had much respect for him, so I got out a piece of paper.

"You want someone with extensive experience, right?" he said. "You need someone good on the phone, someone who has great patience, which you don't have, and someone who can write a complaint and handle basic accounting..."

He reeled off several qualities, and I added a few of my own. In a few minutes, we had quite a list. Someone who could do pleadings with minimal supervision. Someone who knows what interrogatories to send out. Someone who could manage my schedule and on and on. We were looking for a superstar, and I was secretly convinced there was no way we could find someone to fill the bill.

"Now, if you could find someone with all these skills, would you be willing to pay them $50,000 a year?" Steve asked.

I swallowed hard. The going rate for a legal secretary at the time was around $35,000, and I thought Steve was crazy. But he talked through it with me, got me thinking about how someone like this would free up a lot of my time and allow me to go out and find more clients and make more money. If I found the right person, I could delegate a great deal of work to them.

So I put an ad in the statewide law journal. "Looking for a superstar secretary," the ad said and listed all the qualifications I was looking for and set the pay at $50,000. I believed the ad was a waste of time because the person we were looking for did not exist. But I wanted Steve to continue mentoring me, so I played along.

In forty-eight hours, I had 200 résumés from some of the most amazing people you can imagine. One of them was a woman named Laurie Sackett. She had every qualification I was looking for and a few I hadn't thought I needed but did. I was shocked. She was running a small law firm and had twenty-five years of experience. She hadn't been looking for a job, but her firm had a cap on secretary salaries, and she hadn't had a raise in five or six years, so my ad caught her attention.

I hired Laurie, and she worked for me until she retired eleven years later. She was the perfect manager and helped me grow the firm in the coming years. She was my secretary, my office manager, the mother hen of the office. She was worth every penny I ever paid her.

Hiring Laurie Sackett changed my life—and not just because she made my office run much more smoothly, efficiently, and profitably. It changed my life because it showed me how vital it is to look for the right employee and pay them accordingly.

Most law offices don't do this. I took some heat from other lawyers for paying a secretary so much more than the industry average. Still, these are the same firms that cap their key employees' salaries and then wonder why those people leave. I decided I was not going to be cheap with my employees. I decided I would pay my employees more than the market rate and that they would be happy and not leave me. Today, there are lawyers in my firm who make seven figures and our secretaries make way more than they would at other firms.

When you're talking about the things they don't teach you

in law school, this is one of the big ones. Lawyers are clueless when it comes to hiring and paying their employees. I get calls all the time from lawyers who want to know how much I pay our associates or how much I pay paralegals. Lawyers are frugal, for the most part, and they work hard and want to keep what they make. But what I've learned is that when you're generous, your employees work harder. They're more loyal, and your investment in them is returned many times over.

I don't believe for a second that people reading this will drop the book and rush off to give their employees raises. But I do hope I can get you thinking about hiring and paying with a more entrepreneurial mindset.

You have to think about what kind of person you want in your office. Are they a good fit? Do they have the right demeanor? Do their skills complement others who work there? And if they are a good fit, are you ready to pay them accordingly? Steve showed me the value of taking the time to think these questions through, and once again, he was right.

THE TESTS WE USE

Steve also was a big believer in having job applicants take a battery of tests before the interview process. When I first started my law practice about twenty years ago, he advocated tests that measured candidates' IQ, honesty, personality, behavioral tendencies, and cognitive skills.

Although I trusted my ability to interview people, I agreed to give the tests a try. But before I started, Steve recommended I take the tests myself. At the time, I wasn't sure why this was such a great idea. The tests cost over a thousand dollars. That sounded like a waste of money. What was I going to learn?

"You can't be a good business owner until you know yourself," Steve explained. "How will you know if an employee is a good fit for your firm if you don't know what they are trying to fit in with?"

It made sense, but it was still difficult for me to fork over the money to take all these tests. My wife and I did it, however. I hadn't heard of the Wonderlic test or the CBI test, but over about six hours one day we took them all and found ourselves eager to get the results. We got a thorough, 20-page report, and we sat down with the expert to go over the results.

I was stunned by how accurate these tests were. They described me to a tee. It revealed so much about me that I couldn't imagine not using the tests on anyone I was thinking about hiring. When I struck off on my own, I had my first hire take the same tests, and I've used them on every hire since.

WHAT TESTS REVEAL

As far as I know, we're one of the few law firms in the country who ask candidates to take these tests, which are often called assessments. The tests give us incredible insights into how candidates will think, behave, and solve problems on the job.

Some candidates are uncomfortable with testing and don't want to do it. They are afraid to look at themselves, and they don't particularly like others peering into their mind and personality. I understand. But this step in the hiring process is not negotiable. The tests help me get to know the candidate and help me see whether they are a good fit for us. If a candidate declines to take the test, then they can't work at our law firm. It's a nonstarter. I want people who are open to learning about themselves. People not willing to take the tests probably won't be good at constructive criticism, which means they won't be a good fit at our firm.

Our testing procedure increases the odds we'll find the right person. I'd say it doubles our chances, and the odds might be even greater.

We take hiring seriously because we feel that great people are crucial to our firm's success. If you don't start with great people, you can't do anything to get better. You can't coach, you can't mentor, you can't reward, and you can't polish your reputation.

Testing helps you understand someone—how they work and how to best communicate with them. What's their native skill? What distracts or annoys them? Are they great talkers who make strangers feel comfortable? In that case, they might be best for screening calls and evaluating a potential client's claim. Are they thoughtful and detail-oriented workers? Great. Maybe we'll have them help clients write answers to interrogatories. Introvert? Fine. We'll make sure we call on those folks in meetings so we can hear their great ideas.

My first hire, Laurie Sackett, was reluctant at first to do the testing. But after she heard my request and reason, she quickly agreed. Knowing her now as I do, she is a very confident person. She didn't care what the tests showed. She knew who she was, and if I didn't like it, she didn't care.

But I liked what I saw. Each test provides valuable insight, and one thing hers showed was that she didn't like change. This is understandable. Most people don't. So I knew if I changed her duties, moved offices, or amended procedures, I would have to consider Laurie's inclinations. I did. I would explain changes to her in a different way, and this made our relationship solid.

We've even gone so far as to have our best existing employees take tests so we can establish a benchmark against which future candidates are measured.

The best test for measuring cognitive skills is the Wonderlic. This test doesn't say whether an individual is lazy or ambitious or what motivates them, but it will give you insight into their brain and how they process information. If you give candidates only one test, give them this one.

The Wonderlic, like the other tests, is just a step in the process. They never take the place of a live interview. I've interviewed people who test great but were unpleasant in person, and I didn't hire them. I've had people who had low scores on the test, but I loved their personality and work ethic, so I hired them. I don't do that very often, but if you aren't giving any tests, you don't have the option of overriding the results.

We all have horror stories about spending thousands on hiring someone only to have them quit after a week, or steal from you, or smoke pot in the parking lot before coming in for work. Testing doesn't eliminate these characters, but it does make them easier to spot and to avoid.

OVERCOMING OBSTACLES TO TESTING

Many of you will say you don't have time to set up a detailed hiring process or find the best tests to give your job applicants. If that's the case, delegate the job to someone else in your office, such as a secretary or office manager. Around here, I asked my COO, John, to find the best tests and the best people to administer the tests. "Make this process as foolproof as you can," I told him. So if you think you don't have the time, delegate it.

There are a few caveats to consider, too:

⬥ Some employers won't test because they worry about violating the Americans with Disabilities Act (ADA), Title VII of the Civil Rights Act of 1964, or the Age Discrimination in Employment Act. These opponents worry that a failed job candidate might be able to sue for discrimination by showing the personality trait you were screening for is protected under the law.

⬥ According to the Edward Lowe Foundation, Title VII doesn't ban personality tests, but it prohibits you from using tests to discriminate against minorities intentionally. The Equal Employment Opportunity Commission considers a psychological test to be a medical exam under the ADA if it gives evidence of a mental disorder. The ADA can also be a factor if an applicant claims an employer discriminated on the basis of a perceived disability.

⬥ People can cheat on the test. This isn't a concern if you correctly administer the test, but remember that acceptable answers are often a quick Google search away. Some candidates are willing to take that route.

- ♨ Some candidates might be in a temporarily distressed emotional state when they take the test, and the results don't accurately reflect their personality.

- ♨ The tests will often prolong the hiring process, and this alone can cause you to lose a high-quality candidate who has several offers to choose from.

You can avoid these concerns by hiring experts to administer your tests. According to the Lowe Foundation, personality testing is a $400 million industry in the US, so it's not hard to find a testing company to conduct this part of your hiring program. When vetting testing companies, ask them for data that supports the accuracy and reliability of their results. You should also do your due diligence and look into whether any test you're considering has ever been challenged successfully in court.

TESTING FOR EMOTIONAL INTELLIGENCE

And always be on the lookout for ways to refine your process or incorporate new tests. We recently tried out the Enneagram test, which measures emotional intelligence. We haven't incorporated it into our hiring process yet, but I predict that someday two or three years from now, we'll look back and say, "Remember when we hired people without testing their emotional intelligence? How did we manage?"

Emotional intelligence encompasses three abilities: the knack for identifying and naming your emotions, corralling your emotions and applying them to the task at hand, and managing your emotions or the emotions of those around you. Someone with a high level of emotional intelligence is sensitive to others' emotions, and this makes them great friends and colleagues. Also, these skills can be improved with practice.

According to Ronda Muir, author of *Beyond Smart: Layering with Emotional Intelligence*, lawyers often score below average in emotional intelligence. She describes many lawyers as being "militantly rational" but says they can improve simply by regularly recording how they feel and why they feel that way. She even recommends they watch movies on mute so they are forced to read characters' emotional cues.

Studies have shown that attorneys with high emotional intelligence are more successful than those with lower scores. They are better at attracting and keeping clients, for instance, and firms that actively emphasized emotional intelligence training for their lawyers experienced record-setting revenue. Meanwhile, their firms' healthcare costs declined.

So did liability costs. That's because emotionally intelligent lawyers communicate better, thus sidestepping the number one reason why attorneys are disciplined or sued for malpractice.

"Emotional intelligence skills sharpen our abilities to assess risks, understand which ethical standards are appropriate in a situation, recognize when and how others are making ethical decisions and to deal better with the emotional fallout from our ethical choices, especially when ignoring or acting against personal values, which lawyers may need to do in advocating for clients," Muir told the American Bar Association in 2017.

As you can see, emotional intelligence is just as crucial in our business as intellect. We must be able to connect with others. We have to be aware of how we're affecting those around us, whether we are negotiating a settlement, selling a client, or trying to change a subordinate's behavior.

HOMEMADE TESTS AND QUESTIONS

Testing isn't a foolproof process. We still make mistakes in hiring. We hired a person recently who scored well on the tests but was terrible once she got on the job. She didn't fit in at all, and she misled us about her strengths. She couldn't do what she claimed she could do, and we had to let her go. In this case, the tests weren't that helpful. Still, tests help cut down on mistakes—provided you don't rush the hiring process.

The adage "hire slow and fire fast" is another practice worth adopting. Take your time when you vet your candidates.

KEY PERSONALITY OR INTELLIGENCE TESTS

Here are a few of the tests we've used or are considering using.

CBI test: CBI stands for Counterproductive Behavior Index, and it helps identify job candidates who may have questionable behaviors, attitudes, and values. It helps ferret out applicants who are likely to steal from your company, show up late or not at all, or use company time to shop online or surf the internet. Specifically, the test spotlights any concerns about a future employee's dependability, aggressive behavior, substance abuse, honesty, computer abuse, or sexual harassment.

Wonderlic test: The Wonderlic Contemporary Cognitive Ability Test measures a person's learning and problem-solving skills. It asks true-and-false questions such as, "Typing the word 'type-writer' requires only one row of keys on a standard computer keyboard." It also asks simple, logical reasoning questions such as, "At a business meeting of five people, every person shakes hands with every other person one time. How many total handshakes occur?"

Wechsler test: The Wechsler Adult Intelligence Scale, or WAIS, provides a general IQ score.

Enneagram: The Enneagram Institute says their tests identify which of nine Enneagram types a person is. The options range from the Reformer (idealistic, principled) to the Investigator (intense, cerebral, innovative).

Prevue: The Prevue Assessment is based on the ICES Personality Inventory, which measures Independence, Consci-entiousness, Extraversion, and Stability (ICES). Prevue expands on this general-purpose occupational personality question-naire by measuring abilities in the specific areas of numbers, words, and shapes. Additionally, Prevue measures motivation and interests by interpreting a candidate's interest in people, data, or things.

Kolbe index: The Kolbe test reveals a person's instincts and "method of operation." It doesn't measure personality, intelligence, or social style but will spotlight a person's natural abilities and preferences.

Predictive matching: According to Morey Stettner, a management writer and trainer, a common assessment measures how well an applicant's personality would mesh with others in your firm. This "predictive matching" helps find someone who fits in with a preexisting culture. For instance, if your office is an unstructured, creative workplace, you might want to avoid someone who prefers rigid formality.

Dig into their résumé and ask detailed questions about how they like to work and how they handle difficult situations. Make sure they interview with all the people they'll be working with, including those who will report to them. But if you make the wrong hire and learn that the person doesn't live your core values, you have to move quickly to fire them. A weak employee can be a cancer in your law firm; they'll make everyone else work harder, and the resentment will build. Keeping a weak or divisive person on your staff reflects poorly on you as the leader of the company.

We also use job-specific tests. Marc Mendelson, our senior litigation attorney, developed an exercise in which writing candidates are given a set of facts about a case and then have thirty minutes to tell the client's story. Marc provides each candidate the same set of facts, so he has a baseline from which to evaluate people. He's looking for creativity, but he's also ensuring the candidate can do the job.

We have a different test for accounting candidates. It's a basic skills exam that measures a candidate's speed and accuracy. Some are going to work slowly and get all their answers right, and others will work quickly and get a few answers wrong. And then there is the person who whips through the test and gets them all right. When that happens, you know you have a star.

A lawyer needs to be able to think quickly on their feet. I test that by asking an unconventional question just to see how they handle it. The question might seem ridiculous, but the answer can be very revealing.

For example, I might ask, "If you were part of a salad, which ingredient would you be?"

"Well, I'd be the dressing," the candidate replies.

"Why?"

"The dressing holds the salad together, and I'm kind of a peacemaker in my family, and I held my law firm together the last three years when one of the partners came down with cancer."

That's a good answer. Sad story, but the right response because it provides insight.

If the candidate struggles to answer that question, that also tells you something. How is that person going to act when a judge asks a question out of left field or starts yelling at him in front of his client or in front of a jury?

Tests are essential because it's too easy to be fooled by mediocre people with fancy résumés and smooth-talking interview skills. If you surround yourself with mediocre people, you'll have a mediocre law firm. But if you take the time to find great people—people willing to take the tests, seriously answer an offbeat question, or pull together a client's story in just thirty minutes—you will make your life a lot easier and your firm more profitable.

EVALUATING YOUR CANDIDATES' VALUES

A central goal of our hiring process is to determine if a candidate embodies our firm's core values. We educate the applicant about those values, then determine whether the candidate shares them.

We have a set of questions for each core value. One of our values is "Dedicated to winning," so we'll ask applicants to describe a project that they consider to be their most significant career accomplishment. We'll ask them to walk us through the project, describing precisely what they did, how they managed the project, and what their biggest mistakes were.

Some core-value questions are more general, such as, "If you were starting a company, what core values would you want it to have?" Here's another one: "How would you want to receive feedback from your team?" We'll also ask, "Is it better to be perfect and late or good and on time?" Again, there are no right or wrong answers, but the answers do reveal whether the candidate embodies our core values.

Once a year, we review how many people left the firm and under what circumstances. Essentially, we ask, "Was it a good exit or a bad exit?" and we try to identify some take-aways we can use to get better. Bad exits—where someone left whom we wish had stayed—are rare, and the number has gone down in the last ten years. Our turnover is low, and we rarely lose someone whom we dearly wanted to keep. Likewise, we examine the good exits, the ones we are glad about. We Monday morning quarterback the situation to discern what we can learn and how we can spot the issues and take action sooner the next time.

The key to hiring is to know what kind of person you're looking for. To determine that, you must know what your firm stands for. It also helps to know the strengths of all your key players so you can look for someone with complementary skills.

TESTING YOUR STAFF

Testing brings benefits even after a person has been hired. Since we frequently test existing employees—either trying a new test or as a training or leadership exercise—we gain insights that make us better managers. When we see that someone has great skills but isn't able to use them in their current role, we might reassign them. The tests allow us to help people succeed.

Here's another example: We had one manager who was somewhat prickly. We knew her to be a sweet and caring person, but we discovered that she could rub people wrong at times as a defense mechanism. John read over her tests and was able to coach her to become a more effective and likable manager.

John himself benefited. When the leadership team took the Enneagram test, John learned that his secret motivation in life is to be liked. People were surprised at that. They tended to think of John as a cold, calculating Mr. Spock type of personality, and John himself admitted he behaved that way because he thought it was the best for the firm. But as a result of the test, John became more open. It also helped the staff to have a fuller picture of John. His relationships improved when people realized he wasn't using data in an aggressive, calculating way but was only trying to help them. This made his insights more constructive because they were better received.

Neel Doshi, coauthor of *Primed to Perform: How to Build the Highest Performing Cultures through the Science of Total Motivation*, says personality tests are useful as a motivational tool in this way. After someone is hired, you can use the test to explore that person's natural work preferences and identify which part of the job is painful for them.

We use these tests to help our managers, help our employees, and help ourselves. I'm always looking for ways to make myself better—a better leader, manager, father. These tests help us do that.

POSITION DESCRIPTIONS AND PERFORMANCE METRICS

Most law firms don't use job descriptions. A paralegal does paralegal stuff. The administrative assistant does secretarial stuff. That's about as granular as it gets.

In our firm, each position has a job description that details key tasks and expectations and what competencies the person in that position needs to have. In most law firms, especially smaller ones, some responsibilities are unclear. People share responsibility for certain tasks, so when those jobs aren't completed, it's hard to determine who is responsible.

We avoid that by making it clear about everyone's roles

and responsibilities. And each person is measured against a benchmark, either by how their productivity compares to someone doing the same job or how their productivity compares to previous years. This way, we can gauge whether a person's performance is improving or declining.

We also measure the work so we can see when we need to add more people. For example, in a Social Security case, there are a number of steps that have to be completed. Someone has to take new calls, fill out applications, file appeals, do treatment updates, handle hearings, and write briefs. Every one of those things has to be done, and we have those jobs quantified so that we know how much need there is every week for each task. We also know how much each person is capable of doing and what they're actually producing, and when we match those two things up, we can see precisely where we might be falling short.

This is particularly critical when your company is growing quickly. A manager who doesn't track these things might come to you and say, "Our Social Security cases are skyrocketing! We need another paralegal!" Well, do you? In truth, they may need three paralegals or only a half-time position. When you're tracking the workload as well as your employees' productivity, you can see the need and act with confidence to meet that need.

We also use a preventive action report when someone

makes a mistake that we can't allow to be repeated. This gives the employee time to ponder their mistake and write down corrective measures they will take to ensure it never happens again. The simple act of owning the mistake and acknowledging the damage it caused is an effective way of preventing it from happening again.

SETTING SALARIES

Although I've always paid people at the high end of the scale and have had great success finding excellent employees, many of my lawyer friends say they struggle to find amazing people.

All I can say with certainty is that there are a lot of things you can't control, but salaries are not among those things. Use that control to your advantage: find the best people and make sure you are paying them better than most. If not, you are vulnerable to losing your best people.

We use third-party resources to determine the salary ranges for our market and then try to pay in the fiftieth to eightieth percentile. We pay well, but we also hold people accountable to perform well and earn those higher-than-average salaries.

As a result, we rarely lose people because of money. If you're cheap, guess who stays in your employ? The weakest performers stay because they can't get a job elsewhere. Meanwhile, your superstars are leaving for higher salaries from your competitors. If we can prevent that, we do.

INCENTIVES

Salaries are one thing, and bonuses are another. Bonuses are a great way to keep employees focused.

We offer incentives to every employee who works here. We give bonuses for not only performance but also through contests and profit, when permitted. Everyone has an opportunity to earn more. When we hit our annual goals, everyone parties and everyone gets a large bonus. If we come close to the goal but fall short, everybody still gets the party.

A study by the Incentive Research Foundation found that incentives can boost performance from 25 to 44 percent.

WHY INCENTIVES WORK

Profit-sharing and bonus plans are the marks of a company that values its employees. They foster loyalty to the company and are essential to retaining your best staff members. People who work in the mailroom or at the reception desk should have an opportunity to earn more when they help the firm reach its goals. Incentives compel everyone to be an integral part of a team focused on making the business more successful.

Incentives work best when they focus on near-term goals that everyone is aware of. Our Fast Start program, for instance, rewards people who work hard in the first quarter and meet their interim goals rather than waiting until later in the year to complete their work. It's simple and measurable.

Incentives are most effective when the whole process is transparent. Everyone knows what's expected of them and what they need to do to earn the incentive. The scoreboard must be in full view, and everyone must know up front what the rewards will be and how they can earn them.

Many companies who do this well go so far as to ask employees for individual action plans. What can each person do individually to bring the company closer to its stated goal? This brings all kinds of great ideas to the surface. People develop increased efficiencies and look for ways to collaborate better. It's not just about money; people have a good time challenging themselves and watching their progress, and that's good for your firm.

TYPES OF INCENTIVES

Organizations that use incentives typically offer three types of rewards: profit-related pay, performance-related pay, and a share of company ownership. Although the first two have been shown effective in study after study, the third component—shares in company ownership—hasn't been as effective. We don't use that approach, and research reveals why: share ownership can damage job satisfaction and your employees' trust.

There can be some fallout (see sidebar "Potential Problems of Incentive Pay") from the other two as well. For instance, one study in the *Harvard Business Review* found that if you include only a select number of your employees in profit-related bonuses, overall trust, job satisfaction, and loyalty to your firm can actually decline.

That same study also found that performance-related pay can increase the pressure that employees feel. That additional stress can affect their work.

That may be true in some cases, but the pressure some individuals may feel rarely outweighs the benefits of these incentives. This is particularly true when you hire hard-working, competitive, smart, and focused individuals the way we do. Our folks don't mind the additional pressure. They welcome it.

Overall, studies show more and more organizations are using incentives to improve their company's bottom line and their employees' job satisfaction. A 2018 study by WorldatWork, a nonprofit focused on human resource issues, found that 96 percent of the more than 300 companies, nonprofits, and government organizations surveyed used incentives. That's an increase of 2 percentage points from 2015. The amount spent on incentives also increased, and the percentage of employees eligible for incentive pay climbed from 52 percent to 66 percent. Clearly, companies are seeing the value of incentives for improving their profit and employee satisfaction.

OUR APPROACH TO INCENTIVES

When our annual revenue goal is $160 million, giving people $5,000, $10,000, or $15,000 in bonuses for contributing to that success is a no-brainer. I pay bonuses because people deserve them and because it improves our business. Like everything, we've analyzed it; the more I give away to my employees, the more money I make.

John has three principles when it comes to bonus and incentive programs:

- **Don't be greedy.** Spread the wealth around. It acts like fertilizer, making your staff stronger, happier, inspired, and loyal.

- **Be transparent.** Set objective criteria for bonuses, tell people in advance, and let them decide how much of a bonus they want to earn. People don't just receive a bonus; they *earn* it. And this makes them more appreciative in the end.

◊ **Pay on profit, not revenue.** If we paid the team leaders in our office just on gross revenue, they would forever be asking for more resources to get their work done. But when we pay them according to the net profit, they have an incentive to keep costs down. This allows them to decide whether they want to hire more help and earn a smaller bonus or work harder and take home a larger bonus.

HOLDING PEOPLE ACCOUNTABLE

Holding people accountable was one of the biggest frustrations we had in our firm. It was frustrating because our firm is large, and sometimes it's difficult to determine who dropped the ball. Another reason for the frustration stems from my attitude about my company. This firm is my family. I started it from scratch and grew it into something special. You can't do this if you don't treat people right, so I was never big on discipline. Just ask my three daughters.

I come from the school of work hard, play hard. Get your work done, and no one will complain. That works for a smaller firm, where you can't hide in the shadows. When you start to scale, it is much harder to keep track of everything and to figure out who dropped the ball. When you find that person, you must hold them accountable. If you're not willing to hold people accountable, there is no point in developing your core values, tracking data, or establishing internal processes.

POTENTIAL PROBLEMS OF INCENTIVE PAY

If you decide to start, change, or expand your firm's incentive program, there are a few potential problems you need to keep an eye out for:

- **Incentive pay can encourage some employees to act improperly.** A good example is Wells Fargo, whose incentive program encouraged its employees to open bank accounts for customers without the customers' permission. The bank now faces billions in fines and legal settlements—not to mention the customers and trust it also lost.

- **It can increase tension among coworkers.** This can happen when some team members are not as productive as other team members, yet each gets the same bonus.

- **It can increase the pay inequality gap for women.** Women, according to one study, are already paid 17 percent less in base salary than men. That pay gap increases when incentive pay is factored in.

- **The incentive program must be well managed.** Incentive programs require careful planning and execution. According to the Incentive Research Foundation, this process needs to include training and regular communication to ensure employees are doing the right things to contribute to the firm's success. People need to know the company supports them and is treating everyone fairly.

We injected more discipline in our office by using a technique our coach Gino developed called the People Analyzer. If there is an issue with an employee, the leadership team evaluates that person according to each of the firm's core values. The person gets a plus (they embody that core value) or a minus (they fail to embody the core value) or a plus/minus (they inconsistently demonstrate the core value). Anyone who gets any minuses or two or more plus/minuses meets with their team leader to discuss how the employee can better embrace the core values in question.

Thirty days later, we reevaluate the employee. If the employee has deficiencies, they sit down with their leader again to discuss the core values and how the employee can improve. A second thirty-day meeting is set, and if there are any shortcomings at that point, the employee is let go.

This may sound harsh, but it's not. Keeping someone around who doesn't live your core values is a big mistake. It hurts your business, hurts your credibility as a leader, and can diminish the effectiveness of other employees. It doesn't necessarily mean the person who is let go is a bad person or a lousy employee for others. It merely means they aren't a good fit for your office.

Of all the business practices we adopted that first year, this was the hardest for me to accept. I'd been fired myself, and I knew how hard it could be—for the employee and the office in general.

But these rules ensure that everyone is treated alike and that everyone gets time to improve. It is a lengthy, thoughtful process, and it is necessary to keep our office working at a high level. I am still not the best at hiring slow and firing fast. Unfortunately, hanging on to someone who doesn't fit in always comes back to bite me.

SUMMARY

As you can see, we've been able to take a lot of the guesswork out of hiring. We try to hire not only the best person we can find but the best fit we can find. We want someone who not only understands our core values but lives them every day. What's more, we are always looking for people who complement others in our firm—people who are strong and enthusiastic about doing the work that others in our office may not enjoy.

Testing is crucial to this strategy. It's too easy to be fooled by a ginned-up résumé or a candidate who has a knack for taking credit for things others did. The tests give us deep insight into whether a candidate will succeed with us. The tests also give us a head start in understanding how to best communicate with this new employee.

Another key reason we've been able to cut down on turnover—and avoid wasting money, training, and time on employees who don't work out—is with precise job descriptions. Everyone knows precisely what their job is and what they have to do to succeed at that job. Thanks to our tracking system, we can tell who is getting better at their job and who might need more help. We pay well, and we offer generous incentives but only to those who earn it.

Hiring and firing don't have to be a purely subjective decision. If your firm tracks its numbers carefully, decisions like these can become obvious. So let's move on and talk about how to collect those numbers and get them posted on your Legal Jumbotron.

CHAPTER 3

THE LEGAL JUMBOTRON

GETTING A GRIP ON YOUR NUMBERS

I was lucky; I had some people in my life who convinced me to do things differently. My late father-in-law, Steve Radom, was one. He always challenged me to be better.

And one of those areas he felt I needed to improve was my grasp on my firm's numbers.

"How many cases have you signed up so far this year, Michael?" he'd ask when we had lunch together early in my career.

"I don't know."

"How much money in fees have you brought in since January?"

"Not sure."

"Who's the most efficient lawyer in your office? Who turns their cases around the fastest? Who has the highest average settlement? What part of Detroit do most of your traffic accidents come from?"

"Not a clue."

He'd smile and shake his head.

CHECKING THE SCORE

Think back to the last time you attended a sporting event. There was probably a giant screen that displayed the score, time left, timeouts remaining for each team, and other information. It showed pictures of players and their statistics. It replayed key sequences of the action.

It was a jumbotron, and the players and coaches were continually glancing up at it because they needed that information to make sound decisions.

Fans take the jumbotron for granted, but the players and coaches don't. Those numbers are crucial to their success, and without them, the game would be meaningless.

I'm embarrassed to admit it, but before 2007, I was playing without a jumbotron. I was playing the game, but I didn't know the score. I didn't know how many cases I'd signed up in the last month. I didn't know how many settlements I'd have or how long, on average, it took me to complete a case. I was flying blind.

Most lawyers today are in the same boat. When I sit down with them and start asking questions—*How much money will you make this year? How many settlements are you planning on? What's the average turnaround on your cases? What percentage of your cases settle without filing a lawsuit?*—I usually get blank stares or vague, muffled responses.

Lawyers don't know.

If this sounds like you, read on. I'll explain which numbers are vital and how to use those numbers to make better decisions, spot emerging problems, and uncover opportunities to improve your staff. I'll also show you how to use the numbers to increase your revenue.

If you want to grow your firm, you need a Legal Jumbotron.

WHAT OUR JUMBOTRON TELLS US

Our jumbotron, which is actually a collection of spreadsheets, charts, and tables compiled into a weekly

PowerPoint presentation, shows where we stand. It shows how many calls we're getting, how many clients we've signed up, and how many lawsuits we've filed. It reveals if we're on pace to reach our annual revenue targets. It spotlights potential problem areas that need our attention. It's a living, breathing document that is continually updated and reviewed.

These numbers allow you to make better, faster, and smarter decisions. They allow you to take bold action with confidence. A legal jumbotron also serves as an early warning system, like a smoke detector. Usually, when the smoke detector alarm goes off in your house, all you have to do is open a window or put out a smoking candle or something. But if you don't have that alarm, a small problem can quickly turn into a three-alarm blaze.

Here's an example of how our jumbotron helped us.

On January 4, 2018, we set our revenue goal for the firm: $160 million. We didn't pull this number out of a hat. It wasn't a pipe dream. John, my COO, calculated it with some formulas we use to project what our revenue will be. These formulas use our historical trends, and they are highly accurate because we have several years of data. We know how much certain cases pay and how long they take to settle.

Still, members of my leadership team were skeptical about the forecast.

"No way we're going to hit that number," Marc, one of our lead attorneys, said. He bet John that the number would be far less than $160 million.

I had to laugh. In the first few years, I figured John used elaborate guesswork to forecast. I didn't know what his process was, so it all seemed like voodoo or magic to me. But I've become less skeptical about John's forecasting skills because over the years, I've seen his margin of error get smaller and smaller. Every year, as our data increased and he refined his formulas, John's predictions became increasingly accurate. So when John released his forecast that day in January, I didn't bet against him.

Fast forward to December 28. Twelve months later. The end of the year.

An email from Justin, our CFO, arrives in the inboxes of all members of the executive team at the Mike Morse Law Firm.

"Ladies and gentlemen, it is my pleasure to announce that we've hit $160 million in disbursements for the year," he wrote. "Here's a look at the mind-boggling numbers."

Justin attached a spreadsheet detailing exactly how we had managed this number. This was not hocus-pocus. The spreadsheet included not only the firm's goals for the year but also the goals for each of our fifteen teams. It was color coded, so you could see which teams exceeded their goals and by how much and which teams came in under their goal. It was amazingly detailed.

"A shout-out to the Nach, or should I say the wizard of forecasting!" I replied to all. "I assume none of us will ever doubt his numbers again!"

How critical is it to have accurate forecasting like this?

It's everything.

It's not only peace of mind, but it's also confirmation that your numbers are accurate and your process is working. I don't spend a single minute during the year worrying about whether we are going to hit our number. I know we are going to hit it. With that knowledge, I can focus on our future growth and business. I can focus on new client relations, training and mentoring, and consulting with other attorneys who want our help.

I can sleep at night.

STRONG NUMBERS, EASY DECISIONS

Accurate forecasting is one advantage, but there are many other reasons to love your numbers.

Last year, John noticed that a particular type of case required a big investment of time but produced a small percentage of our revenue. Our lawyers spend 30 percent of our firm's total time on these cases, yet these cases only produce 4 percent of our income.

"Whoa," I said. "Are you telling me that we can refer out 30 percent of our cases but only lose 4 percent of our revenue?"

The type of case John identified was smaller personal injury cases under $30,000 in settlement potential. We used to make our living off those cases. But now the average size of our settlements is above $100,000. Did it still make sense for us to spend so much time on these smaller cases? Or did it make more sense to refer them out to skilled, up-and-coming lawyers who specialize in this area? We were already working with several top-notch smaller firms, and many of them would welcome cases like this.

We immediately took steps to ensure we found great attorneys to handle these files. As those cases moved to other firms, we reassigned our lawyers and allocated more time to the cases that generated larger settlements. The average per-case revenue for the firm increased, and we made up for the tiny loss in revenue by decreasing our overhead and increasing our referral income. What's more, the average tenure of our employees also went up. That meant we weren't spending as much on hiring and training people.

Although we moved quickly to make this change, it wasn't a cavalier decision. It wasn't a gut reaction. We carefully analyzed our data to make an easy decision.

We also use the eighty-twenty rule, the Pareto principle. This rule states that 80 percent of your sales will come from 20 percent of your clients. When we did this analysis, it was clear that our most significant cases often involved truck accidents and motorcycle accidents. We now designate those as high-settlement cases. We treat all cases the same when it comes to customer service and great work. All cases get massive attention. However, these complicated truck and motorcycle cases may involve special measures, such as early accident investigations and special experts.

The numbers we track tell us more than what we are making and spending. Our numbers help us improve the work of our employees as well.

For example, a few years ago, during a leadership team meeting, I asked John how much money we had in settlements that hadn't come through the door yet. John tapped the keys of his laptop a few times and then came up with a number: $30 million.

I couldn't believe the number was that high. So I asked John to find out which of our staff attorneys were the best at getting settlements disbursed and which ones took longer than average. In less than a week, he was back with the information.

Most everyone on staff got settlements disbursed quickly, but there were three or four who were slow. Disbursements from their cases went out months after they settled them. I felt our clients deserved better service than that.

Armed with these numbers, we went around the offices, congratulating those who were fast and explaining to the rest why they needed to be faster. If they could get those checks in sooner, we could include them in year-end bonuses. Their clients would have spending money for the holidays. Everyone would be happier.

Who could argue with that?

What's more, we got the attorneys who were good at processing the settlements to share their strategies and procedures with the slow ones. As time went on, the attorneys who used to take three months to get settlements disbursed were improving their times. Today, everyone gets their settlements processed quickly.

This is just one of a hundred different ways we use metrics to solve problems, reduce stress, help our staff, and make decisions. Using data, we can tackle problems quickly when they're small instead of later when they're big. Numbers increase our efficiency, identify employees who need coaching, dictate our advertising, measure performance, and hold staffers accountable.

Before I had a talented COO, I didn't collect numbers like this. I didn't collect any numbers. I was an attorney, for crying out loud. I tried cases. I spotted issues. I negotiated with insurance companies. I didn't know about the average size of settlements for different types of cases or even how long it typically took me to get settlement checks. I didn't care about numbers because I didn't know how valuable they were or how to use them to help me make decisions.

Most lawyers have cases coming in, and they have money to pay their secretary, paralegal, bookkeeper, cleaning service, and landlord. They seem to be doing just fine. But do they make enough to justify hiring another lawyer? Should they expand the size of the office? Should they launch an advertising campaign? Should they start taking Social Security cases or divorce cases? Should they open another location? These questions trouble them because they have insufficient information to make a smart decision.

THE DATA THAT COUNTS

Over the last twelve years, our jumbotron has blossomed from a single page to a ten- or twelve-slide PowerPoint presentation. We review it every Tuesday. The data looks at not only broad, overarching numbers but also at more discrete statistics.

We examine our year-to-date settlements and also how our current year compares to past years. We drill down to look at how each team is doing compared to its budgeted goals, or how much we are making in referral fees. We break our referral fees down by the top six or seven attorneys we refer out to.

We go into that kind of detail because we know how to and because these numbers help us spot problems.

Most law firms don't need that level of detail. But you still need a simple jumbotron and a system for collecting data. You must regularly review the data and make decisions based on it.

As a personal injury firm that works on contingency and not at an hourly rate, here are the essential numbers we track:

🔥 Amount of gross settlements in dollars

🔥 Number of cases that resulted in attorney fees

- 🔥 Amount of net attorney fees

- 🔥 Number of new calls

- 🔥 Number of new sign-ups/clients

- 🔥 Number of cases referred out to other law firms

- 🔥 Income from referrals

- 🔥 Number of lawsuits filed

A one-page jumbotron should list your annual goal for each category, your year-to-date target, your year-to-date actual, and the year-to-date differential. A good jumbotron also lists your weekly goals and your actual numbers for the last three weeks. We also track our number of active files and the settlement amounts that are still outstanding.

The accompanying graphic shows a basic jumbotron, with some sample numbers in it to help illustrate how it works.

Week #13

Data Point	Annual Goal	YTD Target	YTD Actual	YTD Diff	YTD Diff
Amount of Attorney Fees Paid	$1,560,000	$390,000	$405,000	15,000	4%
Number of Attorney Fees Paid	52	13	14	1	8%
Amount of Settlements	$5,200,000	$1,300,000	$1,650,000	$350,000	27%
Number of Settlements	52	13	17	4	31%
Number of New Calls	1040	260	225	-35	-13%
Number of New Sign-Ups	104	26	21	-5	-19%
Number of Cases Referred Out	208	52	40	-12	-23%
Amount In from Referrals	$260,000	$65,000	$92,5000	$27,5000	42%
Number of Complaints Filed	52	13	13	0	0

Actual by Week Number

Data point	Weekly Goal	#13	#12	#11
Amount of Attorney Fees Paid	$30,000	$35,000	$28,000	$30,000
Number of Attorney Fees Paid	1	2	1	1
Amount of Settlements	$100,000	$275,000	—	$95,000
Number of Settlements	1	2	0	1
Number of New Calls	20	16	17	19
Number of New Sign-Ups	2	1	2	2
Number of Cases Referred Out	4	1	2	3
Amount In from Referrals	$5,000	$7,500	$6,000	$8,000
Number of Complaints Filed	1	1	1	1
Outstanding Settlements	$433,333.33	$650,000	$575,000	$550,000
Number of Active Files	150	154	153	155

This jumbotron is a basic Excel spreadsheet with numbers for where the firm stands at the end of the first quarter (week 13) of the fiscal year. Certain cells use formulas to calculate results based on relevant numbers in other cells. For example, when you type in your year-to-date settlement amounts of $1.65 million (row 4, column 4), the spreadsheet immediately announces that you are 27 percent ahead of pace for the year (row 4, column 6).

Nice going!

We can help you set up your jumbotron. Visit www.855mike wins.com/fireproof and enter your contact information. We'll send you a free white paper and a basic Excel spreadsheet that will help you on your journey to setting up your jumbotron. Once your jumbotron is up and running, you'll wonder how you lived without it.

THE PERSPECTIVE YOU NEED

Numbers alone won't help much; you need to put them into context. To do that, compare your weekly snapshot to as many previous weeks as you can so you can spot trends. You should also compare your weekly number to your weekly goal.

It's even more critical to include your year-to-date numbers and your year-to-date goals. Say your firm's goal is to bring in $1.56 million in attorney's fees (see *Annual Goal* in the accompanying graphic). By week thirteen, your target (*YTD Target*) should be $390,000 (row 2, column 3). However, your actual tally (*YTD Actual*) for week thirteen is $405,000 (row 2, column 4). This means you're 4 percent ahead of pace (row 2, column 6). You had a solid first quarter!

You can also spot alarming trends.

In the example, one of those problem areas is in row eight—the *Number of Cases Referred Out* to other firms. According to this table, your firm is 23 percent behind its goal (row 8, column 6). You should have referred fifty-two cases by now, but you've referred only forty.

Now look at the bottom table. These are your firm's weekly numbers. If you look at the *Weekly Goal* column and go down to the *Number of Cases Referred Out* row, you can see you should be referring four cases a week (row 8, column 2). But in week thirteen (row 8, column 3), you only referred out one case and in the two previous weeks, you referred two and three cases respectively.

That's a problem. But *why* is it a problem?

Let's go back to the top table. Row six (*Number of New Calls*) offers a clue. The firm's number of incoming calls is down. The *YTD Target* for new calls is 260 (row 6, column 3), but the *YTD Actual* is only 225 (row 6, column 4). Calls are down 13 percent.

Now go back to the lower table to dig a little deeper. Your weekly goal for new calls is twenty (row 6, column 2). In week eleven (*#11* column), you had nineteen new calls, but in the next two weeks (*#12* and *#13*), you had seventeen and sixteen. Your *Number of New Calls* is trending downward.

You can quickly see how data helps you focus on potential problems. Why are calls down? Is your firm advertising on the wrong TV station? Are callers who leave messages not getting prompt return calls? Is there a new personal injury attorney in town who is advertising heavily and siphoning off some of your calls? Has the receptionist been out on medical leave? Was the temp not properly trained?

Thanks to your jumbotron, your firm can see it needs to focus on its intake process. New calls are down, and sign-ups are down 19 percent year to date. This isn't a reason to freak out and start firing people, but it is a valid reason to talk with the people who are responsible for making the phones ring. You have done well with referral income—revenue is up 42 percent—but that number will plateau or decline if you don't get more calls and more cases to refer out.

On the positive side, the top table shows that the *Number of Complaints Filed* (row 10) is right on pace. You're meeting your goal from week to week and year to date. Whoever is in charge of that part of the business should get some praise. They are running a smooth-operating machine.

SPOTTING TRENDS WITH DATA

Some metrics don't have to be tracked weekly but are smart to have on your jumbotron. These would include:

- 🔥 Money in outstanding settlements

- 🔥 Number of active cases

In the lower table, you can see that your firm's weekly goal for *Outstanding Settlements* (row 11) is $433,333.33. But in week thirteen, you had $650,000 (row 11, column 3), and in the previous week, you had $575,000 in outstanding settlements.

This could mean your attorneys aren't disbursing fast enough—angering their clients—or that you had a recent influx of settlements. Either way, you should drill down and find out why your pipeline is overflowing.

The number of active cases is another valuable metric. We track this weekly. In the lower table, you can see that your firm's goal is to maintain about 150 active cases. That number can float up and down slightly because your staff can flex to accommodate more cases, so the numbers on the right showing that your firm is hovering just above the 150 mark is no cause for concern. It's good news: everyone seems busy!

As you can see, the numbers tell a compelling story. They identify an issue and point you like a compass in the direction of a topic worth exploring. The figures reveal emerging problems as well as smooth-running activities.

But do you have to review your numbers weekly, the way we do?

The answer is yes.

You must collect data every day and review it at least once a week. How long do you want to wait to learn that your number of new clients is steadily declining? I don't want to wait for a second. You can't wait three months or six months, thinking that it will eventually even out, because by then, the problem is much bigger and more costly to solve. What's more, you may find yourself working sixteen-hour days in December in a mad scramble to make your revenue goals.

When the numbers in a particular area drop, you must act. Merely being aware of the number will not fix the problem. For instance, this summer I noticed our referrals from other firms had dropped slightly. It wasn't a dramatic drop, but it was trending downward. So we printed out a list of the firms who have referred cases to us in the last ten years. Then we matched those firms with people in our office who had a past relationship with those firms. Now our attorneys are inviting their attorneys out to lunch, and I'm sure the topic of referrals will come up. We'll remind those firms how much we appreciate those referrals.

The numbers won't provide answers, but they help you find

solutions. They are like a medical checkup that reveals you have high cholesterol. You're not sick yet, but you might want to lay off the fries for a while.

Ironically, the jumbotron doesn't increase your anxiety about your practice. Instead, it gives you peace of mind. I couldn't be more energized than when I look at the jumbotron and see immediately where things are great and where we need to adjust.

GETTING STARTED WITH DATA

It isn't hard to get started. Once you've identified who is responsible for compiling numbers and you've populated your first few jumbotrons, the process becomes more manageable. The key is holding people accountable and then taking the time to review the numbers and act on them.

Follow these steps:

◊ **Designate someone in your office to start collecting the data.** I'm not suggesting a lawyer do this work, particularly if they are the firm's visionary. A small firm should look for someone comfortable with numbers, such as your accountant, bookkeeper, or receptionist. More than one person can collect the data. However, one person should be responsible for compiling the numbers and holding everyone accountable for submitting their information. You can also outsource the job; some people love numbers and will do the work in less time and for less money than someone on your payroll.

⚭ **Use your current systems to cull the data.** Between an accounting system such as QuickBooks and practice management software like CasePacer, all of these numbers are readily available. Otherwise, you'll need to develop a logging system to track the numbers you want.

⚭ **Standardize your data.** If the people typing data into your database spell Detroit seven different ways, this causes problems in getting accurate information. We use drop-down handles in our case management software as a way to avoid typos that can undermine the reliability of your data.

⚭ **If you don't need it, don't collect it.** Focus only on the data that helps you make decisions. You don't need to know that a secretary comes to work on time 98.6 percent of the time.

⚭ **Develop a baseline.** For example, we know about 10 percent of our calls result in sign-ups. We know 45 percent of our claims become lawsuits. We know the average settlement for each lawsuit is presently about $100,000. If we take steps to improve those numbers, we'll compare the new numbers against the baseline to see if our adjustments are working.

♦ **Measure your progress.** If you want to refer out more cases and keep the best, check to make sure your new sign-ups are going down while your referral fees go up. If you want to see if your advertising is effective, track your calls and ask clients where they heard about you.

♦ **Start drilling down.** We also call this "peeling back the onion." Recently, our jumbotron showed that our overall disbursements were fine. However, as we examined the underlying data, we noticed that our first-party litigation was setting a record while our third-party disbursements were below goal. Why? When we peeled back the onion, we learned that several of our most promising third-party litigation cases were on the cusp of settling and we would close the gap in short order.

♦ **Ask questions and use data to answer them.** When you see something happening, dig in to find out why. Say, for example, your amount of money for settlements is good. *Why* is it good? Is it because you have more settlements, or is it because the average settlement is high? If the settlements are higher than average, why? Is there a particular attorney in the office who is doing something great? What exactly is it they do? Is it something they can teach the other attorneys?

◊ **Set key benchmarks.** Benchmarks are what you compare your numbers to in order to put them in context. We make all kinds of comparisons, including:

→ Year-to-date numbers compared to goal and to past years.

→ Attorney to attorney.

→ Team to team. This allows you to spot which teams need help. If one team is struggling with its writing, you might transfer someone from a team of strong writers to the weak team.

→ Market to market. We know that advertising in certain areas produces higher-quality cases than TV commercials running in a different market.

→ Case to case. What type of cases delivers the most revenue? As I mentioned earlier, when we did this analysis, we found a whole class of cases—30 percent of our docket—that didn't return much profit for our firm. We refer those cases out now, but it hasn't affected our bottom line, and we have less stress and better focus.

◊ **Refine your data.** Once you get comfortable collecting and analyzing your numbers, start adding more detail. For example, we average about 450 new calls a week. But what were those calls about? How many were auto accidents? How many were dog bites or motorcycle accidents? What day of the week is the busiest for incoming calls?

🔥 **Be realistic.** Don't expect more than the data can deliver. You have three realities with data: it can be timely, accurate, or stable. You can pick any two, but you can never have all three. Last Tuesday morning, John shared our weekly revenue figure. The data was accurate and timely, but it wasn't stable because one of the secretaries sent in a disbursement that afternoon that she'd forgotten to submit the week before. If I had waited for the late disbursements to come in, the data would have been stable and accurate, but it would no longer be timely.

CHANGING YOUR MINDSET

Many lawyers don't believe the numbers matter. Instead of putting numbers into a spreadsheet, they think their time is better spent finding new cases. They contend that their firm isn't big enough to justify tracking their data.

Data helps everyone, even solo practitioners. Data can reveal when it's time to hire an assistant or find a partner. It can dictate when you need to reach out to bigger firms to seek more referrals. It can measure if you're getting faster with your cases or earning larger settlements.

Other attorneys worry about how their staff might react if they started tracking performance metrics. Would the team feel threatened? Scrutinized? Would people quit?

You don't have to use numbers to threaten people. Instead, use them to identify strengths and weaknesses, areas of improvement and opportunities to restructure so you're ready for any threat or opportunity that comes along.

WHY DATA MATTERS

As I mentioned in the introduction, about ten years ago, my firm was getting most of its cases from another attorney in town. Sid was the biggest advertiser in our market, and for more than a decade, he sent hundreds of cases to us. When we settled a case he referred, we sent Sid 40 percent of our portion of the settlement.

Both firms did well. I built my firm on those cases, and Sid made up to $4 million a year in referral fees from my firm.

Many attorneys would be happy with this arrangement. Cases came in, and we profited.

But the numbers made me nervous. At one point, almost

90 percent of our cases came from Sid. That number was much higher than I anticipated. What if Sid retired or died? What if he sold his firm and the new owners stopped referring cases to us? My firm's pipeline of cases could be cut off at any moment, and where would that leave us?

We were too dependent on one person. All our eggs were in one basket.

Consequently, we set the goal of decreasing our cases from Sid. That may have been what saved us in 2011, when Sid did what I feared: he walked into my office and announced he was no longer sending us new cases.

This was a cataclysmic moment. What were we going to do?

We turned to the numbers for answers.

We calculated that if we put the same amount we paid Sid in referral fees into television advertising, we could get more client calls and rebuild our dockets. So that's what we did. We finished all our existing Sid cases and sent him his referral fees as usual. We started advertising, and as new cases came in from our ads, we kept all the best cases (and the revenue they generated) and referred less lucrative cases to other firms. This generated our own referral income, which we then earmarked for more advertising.

It worked. Today, our referral income pays for nearly all of our television advertising.

Data helps with big decisions, and also with the small, day-to-day decisions. One day, we noticed that one of our teams had 424 cases. When we peeled back that onion, we noticed that the group had 148 cases in prelitigation and 276 in litigation. This team's 34 percent prelitigation caseload was below the firm average of 49 percent. It was imbalanced. This told us that some of the attorneys on that team—our highest-paid employees—wouldn't have enough cases to work on in a few months, so we reassigned some to teams that needed their help.

Here are some other ways data can help you:

◊ **Make cash-flow projections.** Many smaller firms struggle to have sufficient cash on hand to cover day-to-day expenses, from salaries to hiring court reporters for depositions. When money gets tight, some of these firms have to turn to funding companies that make high-interest loans. But if these law firms knew when to expect their revenue, they could plan ahead and avoid the extra expense of borrowing money.

◊ **Inspire your employees.** We hire competitive and confident attorneys who don't mind measuring up to their peers. They *like* being held accountable. Our folks are their own harshest critics; when they see the numbers, it motivates them to work harder. If you're not competitive, that doesn't mean you're a terrible person, but it might mean that you're not a good fit for our firm.

- ◊ **See where your business is coming from.** When we analyzed where our cases originated, we found that Detroit was nine times more important to us than the next city on the list. We identified which zip codes were the most productive. We learned that if we wanted to grow our business, our most receptive audience lived in those areas.

- ◊ **Track your referrals.** Our firm refers out as many as 100 potential cases a week to about twenty other law firms. We carefully track how many cases each firm takes. Most lawyers don't track this sort of thing. They refer out cases and hope one day the money comes in. That's a big mistake.

- ◊ **Help you spot superpowers.** We have attorneys who are fantastic in trials but not skilled in finding and building cases. We have others who struggle in court but are experts at working up cases and dealing with everything until trial. The data shows this clearly. As a result, we set up teams so we have attorneys doing only what they love and are highly skilled at.

We make our detailed jumbotron available to the entire staff so they can go in at any time and see how they are doing. This builds trust. It also gives people a sense of urgency by getting their competitive juices flowing.

FORECASTING AND DATA-BACKED DECISIONS

The process we use for forecasting our budget also relies on data and is just as magically effective. It's based on three pillars:

- The number of cases

- The average value of those cases

- The timing at which the money comes in

For instance, we've learned over the years that all of our cases pay out in a predictable bell-shaped curve. The accompanying graphic depicts several years of data.

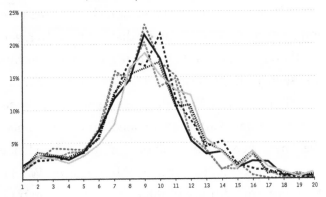

Timing of Disbursements by Quarter Since Opened
(Each Line Represents One Year Disbursed)

As you can see, regardless of the individual case settlement amounts, payout timing is predictable. For the first six quarters after a case is opened, the money trickles in. Then the bulk of the settlements flow in for the next four or five quarters.

This pattern is crucial to our budget forecasting. Another critical piece is our average settlement. An analysis of the thousands of cases handled by our firm since 2009 showed that the average settlement is a hair under $106,000. John takes all this data, puts it into his forecasting model, and predicts our financial outlook for the coming year. We've become so good at this that we can predict to within one-tenth of 1 percent how much our firm will make for the year.

This forecasting also makes it easy to plan for growth. If

I tell John that we want to grow 20 percent by 2023, he can calculate the timeline and come back to me with the information we need to make that happen. To reach our goal, we'll have to have an X increase in new calls by such and such a date, and we'll need a specific number of additional intake staff. By X date before 2023, we'll need to hire X number of attorneys to handle the additional cases. We'll need a certain number of sign-ups, and we'll need to refer out a certain percentage of those cases. We'll need X amount of additional office space and an extra copy machine by such and such a date.

To plan growth like that, you need the data and you need a budget.

John will tell you this forecasting is easy and not particularly impressive, but I don't know of any other law firms that know how to do it. If it's something you'd like to learn more about or try for yourself, go to www.855mikewins.com/fireproof to find out how.

GAINING CONFIDENCE

Spending a little bit of time collecting data can save you a ton of time and anxiety.

For instance, we noticed several years ago that the first three months of each year are slow. Everyone in the office is fat and happy after the holidays, and the first quarter moves at a sluggish pace.

To reverse that, we launched our Fast Start contest. Between January 1 and March 31, we award points and pay bonuses to people who accomplish certain things. These cash awards are in addition to their year-end bonus. People can score points just for doing their regular work and completing it in the first quarter rather than later in the year. Lawyers in our office can make an additional $20,000 to $40,000 in the first quarter just by doing their jobs and staying on pace in those three months.

And it works—every year. Everyone in the office loves it! John and I love it because it prevents a slow start and the need to catch up for the rest of the year. When you have a good start, you have a good year. You have less stress and uncertainty. The $250,000 we pay out in bonuses is an inexpensive way to ensure we have a smoother, less stressful year.

Any lawyer in any type of practice can benefit from data. Divorce lawyers, for instance, should know how many husbands they've represented versus how many wives, and which kind of case brought the best settlement. How many went to arbitration, and how many went to trial? How many had child-support issues, and how many had property issues? How long does it take for disbursements?

Or say you're a criminal defense attorney. Eighty percent of your cases are drunken driving cases, and you do well with them, making $2,500 or $5,000 a case. But what about those personal protection order cases that pay less? How much time do they take, and would you be better off focusing exclusively on the drunken driving cases? If you don't have the data, you don't know.

Remember, I'm not suggesting that lawyers be in charge of collecting this data. If you're like me and you're the visionary in your firm, you'll want to assign this task to someone else. Your job is to hold that person accountable and to make sure the numbers are used in your decision-making.

In our personal injury practice, we track how many cases involve motorcycles and how many involve autos and trucks. How many turned into disability claims? We track all of this because the data helps us advertise better, market better, and to think better. It helps us decide what kind of people to hire, when settlements will appear in our bank account, and when our pretrial expenses are going to be the highest.

The point is that we are confident all year that we will wind up exactly where we predicted we would. That confidence gives us not only peace of mind, but it also enables us to make bold moves when we need to.

We make decisions every day about marketing, advertising,

budgeting, hiring, and resources, and we can make those decisions before problems emerge because the numbers show us the way. We make quick, smart, and bold decisions without second-guessing ourselves or losing sleep at night.

SUMMARY

Don't put off developing your jumbotron. Take the time to start collecting and analyzing your firm's data. It may seem daunting at first, so start out with simple measurements and get comfortable working with the numbers. Track your time, your phone calls, your revenue, your expenses. Look at it over time and compare to similar periods in the past. Is your first quarter always slow? Is your fourth quarter always hectic? Get a handle on your trends, and use the numbers to spot potential problems.

As your data grows and becomes more sophisticated, the decisions you once agonized over will come into sharp relief.

I no longer fear the future the way many lawyers do, not knowing where their next case is coming from. Anyone reading this has felt that uncertainty and anxiety. The simple truth is that there are certain things you can control and certain things you can't, and the numbers help you determine which is which.

Numbers, as you can tell, are central to how we run our

business. But they are just part of our philosophy. To run your law firm like a high-functioning operation, you must adopt many other business practices. To do that, you need to manage your entire law firm the same way you manage your most significant cases.

Read on to find out how to do that.

CHAPTER 4

—

RUN YOUR BUSINESS LIKE YOUR BIGGEST CASE

MAKING EXPERT EXECUTION A CONSTANT

One day, a new client walks into your law firm, and you quickly realize that this will be a big case. This case is not only going to make you a lot of money; it's going to make you famous. It will bring in a hundred new cases and could change the way you operate for the next decade or more. We've all had those cases, and those who haven't had them dream of getting one.

What do you do when that case comes in? Do you toss it to an associate and say, "Bring me a check at the end of the case"?

No, of course not. This is the case of the decade, maybe of a lifetime. To win it, you'll need to be prepared. You'll have to set goals, determine who is going to work on it, and what they will do. You must establish a timeline with milestones, and you have to have a system to ensure you don't miss deadlines. You actively stay in charge.

Sounds exciting!

So why don't you run your law practice like this every day?

What's bigger than your biggest case? Your law firm. Your business. So why wouldn't you be as deliberate about working on your business as you are about working on your biggest case?

You can, and you should. But if you want to bring that kind of high-level urgency, preparation, and execution to the day-to-day operation of your firm, you'll need to adopt some key business practices.

HOW TO ACHIEVE EXPLOSIVE GROWTH

Our work convinced us to adopt a few other business practices that most law offices never use. Along with our core values, these practices formed the launchpad for the explosive growth our firm soon enjoyed. They included:

SETTING GOALS

Years ago, when my father-in-law suggested I set specific goals for my law practice, I was not convinced they were needed. I didn't have any particular goals for the firm. I'd never set goals. They seemed meaningless. Goals were just a number. Besides, you can't predict how many clients will walk through the door or what kind of cases they'll bring. You can't predict settlements. The firm is going to make what it's going to make; why waste time on goals?

Again, I was wrong. When our business coach also stressed the value of specific goals—echoing the words of my late father-in-law—I started to accept this as a good idea.

Today, I can't imagine operating without goals. Much of our success results from having goals.

We have targets for everything—number of calls, number of gross settlements, number of cases, annual revenue. We set goals for the firm, for teams in the firm, for members of the teams. These objectives are our motivation. We set long-term goals and short-term goals, and the tasks we assign every quarter are all designed to keep us moving in the direction of these targets.

And these goals are carefully calculated. They're not pie-in-the-sky goals. We base them on formulas we've developed that take into account our historical data, the capacity of our people, our marketing efforts, our referrals, and the size of cases we are already working on. We've figured out key averages that allow us to set realistic, yet still ambitious, goals.

Few law firms set financial or business goals, but our firm sets several. We have three-year goals, annual goals, even quarterly goals. We set most of our goals with great precision and we track our progress toward reaching them. We know, for instance, that this year we need to sign up 1,820 cases to sustain our growth. Most law firms set out to "sign up as many clients as we can this year," but we have pinpoint goals. We want 1,820 cases, and we want their average value to be 15 percent higher year over year. Our goals are precise and measurable. Ask me on July 15 how I'm doing, and I will be able to tell you to the moment how much progress we've made toward both those figures.

THE THREE-YEAR GOAL

A three-year goal is less precise than an annual or quarterly goal because too much can change in a longer time frame. New laws can be enacted, for instance, and key personnel can change. The world around you can change dramatically in three years. But you still need a three-year goal and a plan for reaching that goal.

Here are some examples of items that might be in a three-year goal:

- All employees are working in small teams focused on discrete areas of the law we practice.

- Our income from referrals will grow enough to offset our advertising expenses.

- Every employee is an A player, doing the work for which they are best suited.

- We are the best place to work among all law firms in Michigan.

- We increase our charitable work by 25 percent or more.

Again, this is not a concrete concept. It's an image of where we want to be, and we use it as a guide when we work on more immediate challenges and when we set priorities.

THE ANNUAL PLAN

Every January, my leadership team and I sit down with Gino and establish our goals for that year. A goal without a plan is just a wish.

These are more tangible than our three-year goals. We look at our staffing. We set specific revenue goals. We'll also set goals for how many calls we want to take, or what areas of law we might want to expand into. We have budget discussions. I am able to brainstorm and use my visionary superpowers to share where I see the firm going.

Many of these goals are measurable and numbers based, and each might require different strategies to achieve. For instance, if our goal is to maximize the value of each case, we may decide we need a better system for reviewing prospective cases to measure their earning potential.

As with the three-year goals, it's vital that we share the annual plan with our entire staff to ensure their buy-in. You want to ensure everyone has a stake in your success and that everyone is rowing in the same direction.

STRUCTURING YOUR OFFICE

Lawyers just starting out learn to be jacks-of-all-trades. They write, research, take client calls, go to court, argue motions, review medical records, interview doctors, do the trials, figure out the bills, keep the client happy, and run their office. They market to get more cases. They study new laws, attend seminars, meet with referral sources. They pay the bills and make sure the postage machine has stamps.

This is how I operated for years.

Even bigger, more experienced firms operate in a similar way. Each attorney has their own office with a secretary. If they're lucky, they have a paralegal. You get your files, and you do the work, and the secretary kicks it out. You live on this little island. You have little opportunity to strategize with other lawyers, and as we mentioned earlier, high-priced attorneys are forced to do things that lower-paid people can do just as well, if not better, than you.

This dawned on me after I hired Laurie, my superstar secretary. She not only enjoyed doing many of the things I disliked doing, but she was also better at them than I was. This was a revelation. She immediately gave me more time to work on cases, which is what I loved doing and was one of the best at.

This was my first experience with delegating. I started looking for more efficiencies.

TAKING A TEAM APPROACH

When I realized Laurie was spending a couple of hours a day at the copy machine, I suggested we hire a part-time person at $10 an hour to do that. She loved the idea, and it freed her to spend more time on work that produced revenue for the office. Soon, she had help with the copying, answering the phones, and running errands, and we had fewer things pulling us away from working on our clients' cases.

Still, as our office grew, we had a traditional office structure:

each attorney had one secretary. We hired paralegals to assist as well. We also had a presuit team that worked on the case with the clients. When the case was ready to litigate, the clients said goodbye to their presuit team and were assigned a litigation attorney. This was efficient, but when we instituted client surveys and reviewed the feedback we got, we noticed that some clients felt like they were being bounced around too much.

In 2012, John and I developed the team system we use today. We created individual teams, each of which had lawyers, secretaries, and paralegals assigned to it. They were like their own mini law firm. The client meets their team, including their lawyer, at the outset and stays with them throughout the process. The paralegals assist with running the process at first, but the litigation lawyers are involved from the start and are available to the client anytime for questions. The attorneys direct and train the paralegals, and they meet face-to-face with the client every ninety days.

This system clicked. We eliminated our number-one customer complaint. Not only has client satisfaction gone up, but we have fewer clients leave us, and the average value of our cases has gone up.

FINDING THE SWEET SPOT

The teams have succeeded on several levels. For instance:

- 🔥 **Employees love them.** Being on a smaller team gives them an emotional connection to their coworkers. They work harder because they don't want to let the team down. They feel vital and important. They don't feel like a small, autonomous cog in a big machine.

- 🔥 **We can allow top performers to stay in their wheelhouse.** We have three specialty units headed by people who were previously partners in big law firms. They work only in the areas they love. One of our attorneys loves doing trials, and he's practically unbeatable, so he does trials all the time. We have another attorney who has a knack for facilitating cases, so that's what she does for us. Another person previously wrote appeals for insurance companies but now does appeals for us. These are high-powered, skilled people who have made our firm a lot of money by having the freedom to do what they love.

- 🔥 **We can compensate for weaknesses better.** When we set up our teams, we examine each person's strengths and weaknesses so that we can minimize their shortcomings and exploit their powers. If I have a lawyer who tends to procrastinate, I give him a secretary who will hold him accountable and make sure he makes his calls. Some lawyers don't like to try cases. Well, guess what? We have five or six who love to do that and are great at it, so we'll let those people handle the trial.

- 🔥 **It gives you flexibility.** Right now, we have ten teams. We used to have fifteen. We're frequently changing and moving people around as cases develop and workload shifts. We also fold teams into other teams if we realize that an attorney leading a team is not a skilled manager. That's okay; we'll let them do something that they're great at and enjoy.

- 🔥 **They help you focus your training.** All our team leaders get the training they need to be effective managers. They read books, attend trainings, and get coaching on how to get the most out of their people. When you have the right people in the right seats, they bring tremendous insights to their teams and to the firm in general.

- 🔥 **They create internal competition.** We've already mentioned how we use our jumbotron to measure our progress toward our annual goals. The numbers—settlements, cases, lawsuits filed, and so on—for each team are all reported publicly on the same slide, and this motivates teams to accomplish more. They can instantly see how they stack up—who's ahead and who's catching up. Since one of our core values is "Dedicated to Winning," we have hired people who have a competitive spirit and love this kind of rivalry.

- 🔥 **There's no room to hide.** We set up the teams with basic components: a team leader who is also an attorney, a presuit paralegal, a secretary, and a litigation writer. It's clear what each person's responsibility is. If Anna doesn't get the prelitigation work done, we'll know it. Then we can either coach her, replace her, or otherwise get her some help. No one can lurk in the shadows doing mediocre work.

🔥 **The teams are self-governing.** A team's success is measured by its profitability. Its profit determines the team leader's bonus. If the team wants to add resources, such as another writer, the cost of that person comes out of their profit and reduces their bonus. In this way, their compensation is a measure of their efficiency. It's like an internal market force that ensures they aren't asking for unnecessary resources and aren't going to tolerate people on the team being unproductive.

One pitfall of the team system is that some of the lawyers you ask to lead teams have no management experience. They joined your law firm to be lawyers, not managers. Even after receiving training, some of these lawyers aren't cut out for management and get reassigned. Other lawyers love managing and quickly learn how to motivate their people and hold them accountable. Team leaders are rewarded for their good work: they get more time off, more money, and more autonomy.

The team system has helped us recruit some great lawyers

to the firm. We've hired solo practitioners who just wanted to have colleagues to brainstorm with. We've hired people who managed entire law firms and came here because they were at a point in their lives where they wanted to downsize. So they come to work with us and manage a few people instead of an entire firm, and they don't have to do all the HR and accounting that they used to be responsible for.

FAIRNESS AND CONSISTENCY

The bottom line is that the more money a team gets for their cases and the fewer resources they need to get that money, the more team leaders can take home. It all depends on how hard they work and how motivated they are. It's the best way to compare lawyers to each other in a fair and consistent manner.

Say you're an attorney in a traditional law office, and your paralegal and secretary spend thirty minutes every Monday morning talking football. You might be irritated by that, but it doesn't hurt you directly, so you might not say anything.

But if the attorney's compensation is based on the profitability of their team, they might look at that thirty-minute conversation differently. If the team leader is going to have to pay the two kibitzers overtime because they wasted a half hour, the team leader is more motivated to act and ask the football fans to discuss the Lions' wide receiver problems after work over a beer.

I recently had a team leader come to me requesting to hire more people. I looked at the team's numbers and dockets. Compared to what my workload used to be and compared to what the other teams were getting, I realized that this team leader had plenty of people.

"You could do more with what you have," I told him. "Your people aren't working hard enough."

I showed him the numbers and how his team compared to others.

"If you owned your own firm and I came to you with a hundred files tomorrow, what would you say to me? Would you turn them down because you don't have enough resources?"

"Hell, no," he said. "I'd figure out how to make it work."

"That's the right attitude," I replied. "Go figure it out."

And he will. He's smart, he gets it, and he's going to have to go back to his team and have some hard conversations. Everyone will have to work harder. They'll have to figure it out.

And I won't. The structure takes a lot of pressure off me. I don't have to go in and micromanage a team to ensure it's working efficiently.

Not everyone reading this works in a law firm with 150 employees and ten individual teams. But the approach and the principles apply whether you have one team or twenty-seven teams. Teams help you provide great customer service. They make you more efficient. They create an incentive and promote accountability. They give employees a stake in the firm's success, and this keeps them motivated and inspired. People are rewarded for their results, not merely for punching a clock.

CONSISTENT PROCESSES

Although employees have a lot of latitude for managing their teams, they are expected to follow our company's procedures. We have a step-by-step description of every significant process in our office, from how our intake procedure works to how we handle cases. We have dozens of these procedures, and we regularly update them. Everyone is expected to follow them.

People can't say they didn't know how to do something because everything we do is documented. Because our procedures are so thorough, we've been able to inject them into CasePacer, a case management software, so that the second someone completes a task, a reminder pops up about the next step in the sequence.

Documented procedures are the best way to reduce mistakes and increase everyone's efficiency and speed. It's easier to delegate a task when the work has been documented, and the steps are explained clearly. You can also scale up easier when you have documented procedures that new teams can follow as they expand their workload. The clients will appreciate it, too, when they see your procedures are clear and consistent. Procedures manuals are especially crucial for smaller firms where there is usually one trusted assistant who knows everything. If that assistant quits or is absent for an extended period, it could leave your office susceptible to damaging mistakes.

ORGANIZING YOUR OFFICE MANUAL

Most law office manuals have two distinct sections—office policies (its rules and regulations) and office procedures.

The office policy section includes employment, behavior, and such things as inclement weather procedures. The procedures section documents administration functions, such as file management, conflicts-of-interest checking, managing the trust account, calendaring, opening mail, answering phones, and a host of other routine activities. According to Lawyers Mutual Liability Insurance, having these processes and policies documented is vital to prevent malpractice claims and grievances.

The manual should also include a description of your office structure, the building layout, job descriptions, the location of supplies and equipment, shredding policies, and emergency-response plans. Great firms include guidelines for dealing with clients, including:

- How to greet clients and answer the phone

- Office procedures for engaging or declining representation

- The correct use of engagement, nonengagement, and disengagement letters

- Etiquette and timeliness of correspondence and responses

The policies section should document relevant rules and regulations. Many state and federal laws require employers have formal policies for equal opportunity employer, non-discrimination, confidentiality, and privacy. Include your office procedure for harassment in this section.

Personnel policies cover terms of employment and should comply with state and federal employment laws. You'll want to describe your process for employee evaluations, probationary periods, and disciplinary and termination procedures. Lawyers Mutual recommends that you avoid any kind of language, such as "guarantee," that limits your rights as an employer. You don't want any language that might suggest to a judge that this manual is a contract.

Some firms have a section for employee behavior. Here, you can cover your rules about employees' use of social media, blogging, and email. You can also set out who's allowed to represent the firm before the media and who can sign contracts on behalf of the firm. You can also establish a dress code and rules about workspace appearance and maintenance.

SETTING THE RIGHT TONE

You don't want your office manual to come across as harsh and punitive. You want to project a warm and welcoming tone, since the manual will likely be used most often by new employees. Don't hit them with all your rules and penalties. Instead, keep it positive, upbeat, and supportive.

It's also vital that the manual be written in simple language. Use a lot of bullet points so it's a document that is easy to scan as a reference. Keep your paragraphs short, and don't let sentences go beyond twenty words. You want busy people to be able to quickly find what they are looking for and absorb the key points at a glance. You want people to be glad they chose to work at your firm. You don't want them to feel buried under an avalanche of brutal restrictions and warnings.

It took us a year to get all our processes documented, and we revise them as laws change, new software is introduced, or new best practices emerge.

When we notice someone is faster at a procedure than others, we incorporate the efficient person's methods into our procedures. For instance, if highly productive Julie uses eight steps to finish a job whereas Kate uses ten, we'll update our processes to reflect Julie's approach. This way, we elevate everyone's game and increase our overall efficiency.

These procedures are not only a great training tool for new employees but also a great accountability tool. It's clear when someone takes a shortcut. On the other hand, anyone from outside the team can step in, call up a case, and see what stage it's in. So it's a great communication tool as well.

GETTING STARTED WITH DOCUMENTATION

Many of you are probably dreading the job of documenting your office's processes. This kind of work is unsatisfying to many creative people. If it sounds dull and uncreative to you, then delegate the job to a secretary or paralegal who relishes doing detailed work.

If you're doing this yourself, start with a brain dump of all your regular processes. Just open a blank Word doc or a Google doc and start a comprehensive list of each routine task that would benefit from a how-to document. If you don't want to spend time in front of a computer screen, dictate your procedures and steps into your phone and send the recording to a transcription service. Another option is to acquire a sample, generic manual and edit it to your liking.

If you're delegating the job, have your assistant interview you about your procedures and write the process for you to review. Break each core process into the basic steps, and have a few people follow them to determine if they are clear. Tweak any areas that seem vague or incomplete to the beta user. Start by documenting the most common practices and then build your collection of procedures over the next several months. Keep it simple. Here are a few other tips:

- 🔥 **Start with why.** Explain in an introductory paragraph when this process should be used and why it is critical. This frames the work in a way that reminds the user to use care and attention to detail.

- 🔥 **Employ flowcharts.** Some people are visual learners, and flowcharts help them see each step in a process.

Flowcharts can also use shapes to convey key steps. An elongated circle is used as the starting point, rectangles represent instructions, and diamonds indicate where a decision has to be made.

🔥 **Make checklists.** Pilots use them. So can you.

🔥 **Get the staff's help.** Have office staff record their activities and write down the steps they take to perform these duties. Review calendars for monthly and yearly tasks and record the actions necessary to complete these activities as well.

🔥 **Simplify.** Avoid going into too much detail on the specifics by repetitively describing the steps for specific document creation when all document creations are essentially the same.

🔥 **Layer your procedures.** For complicated procedures that involve steps and substeps, use boldface and indents to create a hierarchy so users don't get lost.

The best way to document your processes is to start small and keep adding to your collection over time. You can make it available in both a printed binder and a searchable, online database. You can also share the files using Google Docs, Dropbox, or Box. Some procedures might best be documented by creating a short video.

Periodically review your procedures to ensure they're still accurate. Appoint one person to be accountable for seeing that your manual is kept up to date, but charge everyone in your office with the responsibility for looking for ways to improve the procedures themselves. When new employees have a question, direct them first to the manual to ensure it becomes everyone's habit to consult it.

Now that we have all our procedures documented, I can't believe that I kept all this information locked in my head so long. In the early years, people were constantly asking me how to do one thing or another.

Not anymore.

THE OFFICE

Your office design is as important as how you design your teams. In ours, all the teams sit together. We don't have all the attorneys in one area and all the secretaries in the secretarial pool. The lawyers' secretaries and paralegals sit in proximity to one another so it's easier to collaborate. Also, everyone has a private office, even secretaries. It's unusual for a law firm to pay extra to give everyone an office, but we think it's crucial to give everyone an environment where they can feel professional, focus on their work and their phone calls, and be happier.

One mistake most lawyers make—we've made it our-selves—is not getting enough office space. If you're an entrepreneurial attorney who wants to use the ideas in this book to scale your firm, make sure your office has room to grow. Plan ahead and get a space that will suit your needs five years from now. Never sign a five-year lease on a place that fits your current size because in two years, you'll be wishing you had more room.

We have an entire floor of a beautiful building—30,000 square feet. When we moved in here, it was more room than we needed, so we sublet some of the office space. We've since had to take all the space back.

Keeping everyone on the same floor helps ensure a con-sistent office culture. When our teams were spread over different floors, multiple cultures bubbled up. Teams located in different buildings often developed their own subcultures and different ways for handling customers. But now that you can take a lap around the office and see every-one in the company, you can see we have one consistent look and feel.

We have ten conference rooms, and we made that invest-ment so we could cut down on the travel time our attorneys spend to go to another firm for meetings. We have the meetings in our office, which allows our staff to remain productive right up until their meeting starts. There's no downtime in the car or waiting in a reception area for a meeting to start. We've found that the money we save from decreasing wasted time more than pays for the conference spaces we've created.

The conference rooms are also right by the reception area, so clients meeting with their attorneys don't have to come behind the scenes to where everyone is working. We chose a building that was centrally located and highly visible, with an enormous parking lot. Clients don't have to worry about finding a parking spot, and we have many spots by the front entrance reserved for our clients' use.

These are all crucial considerations for attorneys thinking of moving to a new office. You want to plan for your growth, the comfort of your staff, and the convenience of your clients. Get a place that's easy to find, safe, and near plenty of free and safe parking.

THE RECEPTIONIST

Take time to set up your lobby the right way. You want the best person you can find to sit at your front desk, greeting people as they come in!

About fifteen years ago, my wife and I were eating at Fuddruckers restaurant, and we had the most wonderful, outgoing, and attractive waitress I'd ever met. She was perfect—attentive, service-oriented, friendly, and smart. Her name was Jami.

My wife leaned over to me and said, "She'd make a great receptionist at your firm." I agreed and asked her to call me to discuss a potential job.

Had she ever worked at a law firm? No.

Had she ever worked a phone line? No.

Could she type? Not well.

It didn't matter. I hired her. She had that "it" factor when it came to customer service.

She's still with us, and I get more compliments about her from our clients than for anyone else in the office. She remembers everyone's name. She's the first person people see when they walk into our lobby, and she makes everyone feel valued. We've freed her up from answering the phones so that she can be our full-time customer service manager and in-person greeter. People who come in aren't left standing around while the receptionist is on the phone.

Although you may not put as much thought into hiring a receptionist as you would in hiring an attorney, having a great receptionist is crucial to your firm. Your receptionist must personify the image you wish to project. And while they don't need a law degree, they must be knowledgeable about the work you do and all the different steps in the process. Your receptionist often provides clients their first impression of your firm, so you need a receptionist who is confident, capable, and clear-minded about what the client needs.

Here are some additional tips for hiring a receptionist:

🔥 The person's conduct is just as crucial as their credentials. Experience and skills are key. You don't want a receptionist who is nervous or timid. The client is likely nervous or apprehensive already, and the receptionist's job is to be warm and reassuring. Trust your gut on this one: if a receptionist candidate makes you feel relaxed and confident, chances are they will have the same effect on your clients.

🔥 Avoid people who are just looking for a foot in the door. While it's great to have a receptionist with ambition for higher things, you want someone who treats the work like a professional and not like someone biding their time till something better comes along.

🔥 Give them time to adjust. Even the best receptionists need a break-in period, so give them a month or two on the job before reviewing their performance with them.

You can also bring someone in on a temporary basis to see if they're a good fit before hiring them permanently.

MEETINGS

Our meetings are an essential part of our efficiency and productivity. Before we adopted most of our business practices twelve years ago, we rarely had meetings in my office. Everyone was too busy to have a meeting. We'd have them once in a blue moon, and it was usually because some big issue had blown up and we had to address it. Our meetings were a reaction to a problem.

Now our meetings are designed to spot those problems before they even arise.

We use our meetings to ensure everyone understands their role and to hold people accountable. If you promise you're going to do something or if you are assigned a task, your team lets you know they depend on you. This provides clarity, saves time, and ensures healthy communication. People are not expected to merely attend these meetings; they are expected to bring their attention, energy, sharp questions, and willingness to help. Cell phones are off or are not in the meeting at all.

You can have a great vision for your company, but if people don't understand their role in achieving that vision, everything falls apart and becomes mushy. You don't get where you want to go.

We use meetings to ensure we are all headed in the right direction and working together to get there.

MEETING PULSE

Everyone in our firm is in at least one meeting each week. Each team within the company has a standing weekly meeting. They start on time, and they end on time. If you have a long agenda or a particularly meaty issue to discuss, you schedule extra time for the meeting, and you stick to the time you allotted. This is so people don't worry about a sixty-minute meeting stretching into two hours or something like that. They can plan their day.

It's also important to have a regular cadence for your meetings.

We start with an annual meeting where we set our goals for the year. For each annual goal, we establish interim ninety-day targets designed to keep us moving and on pace to achieve that annual goal. Those ninety-day efforts are called rocks—things that have to be accomplished over those thirteen weeks if we are to achieve our annual goal.

After the annual meeting, we schedule quarterly meetings

in which we check to see how people did on their ninety-day rocks. That quarterly meeting is also designed to determine what rocks need to be assigned for the coming quarter. The human brain is wired to stay on course for ninety days but will veer off course over a longer period, so these quarterly sessions keep people from losing sight of our overarching annual goals.

At our weekly meetings, we also discuss our "to-do" assignments. These are assigned weekly, and we follow up at these meetings to see how people are progressing on these assignments.

This is why our meetings are vital. They have specific agendas, and the expectations for everyone are clear. Everyone is assigned rocks or to-dos—either in service to their team or in service to the company in general—and we use the meetings to monitor progress, spot delays, or help people who are struggling.

People who work here must be willing to set rocks and to-dos, and they must be willing to follow through and be held accountable. It's not that complicated. Anyone uncomfortable with our meetings and our expectations is probably not a good fit for our culture. At the same time, we've found that good employees love to be held accountable. They are excited about this approach because it allows them to share their contribution.

STAYING ON TRACK

The quarterly all-staff meetings help our employees buy into our process and fortify their trust.

Unless you're a partner, most law firm employees have no idea what's going on. They don't know if the firm is profitable or struggling, and they don't know what the goals of the firm are. They don't know what would make the firm successful or unsuccessful. They know nothing, and this makes people suspicious, resentful, and distrusting.

We treat our people with respect and openness not seen in most law firms. Every quarter, I stand up in front of everyone and tell them how we did in the last quarter and how we're doing for the year. I share whatever struggles we may be having. We are transparent about our work, our business, and the part each person plays in our office. Employees get a sense that they are on a team that works together and helps each other out. We have each other's back.

During my presentation, I go over our goals for the next quarter, what new initiatives are on the horizon, and whatever challenges we're grappling with. I use this time to teach and explain why we are moving in a certain direction or why we implemented a new policy. My goal isn't to force new directives on people but to help them understand the underlying reasons behind any major decision.

Done right, these meetings are exciting and empowering. Our people feel a part of something bigger than themselves. They own it. As a company, the time we spend preparing for these meetings and holding them is a great investment when compared to the cost of being disorganized or having inconsistent or disjointed communications with the folks who work here.

In addition to these annual and quarterly meetings, each manager in our office has a quarterly one-on-one with each of their direct reports. These meetings are opportunities for the manager to give constructive feedback, review any problems, or talk about future opportunities the employee might be interested in. The meeting also gives employees a chance to give feedback about how things are going from their perspective.

The key to reducing turnover and increasing employee satisfaction is to keep people informed and to listen to what they have to say. Listen more, speak less. That's our mantra. During these quarterly one-on-ones, which are usually held outside our offices, we want our people to have the opportunity to talk about what's good and what isn't working as well as it should.

Executives on our leadership team also make it a point to sit in on weekly team meetings. They're there to answer questions, but mostly the executives observe. They want to ensure the teams are having helpful conversations, following company processes, and holding each other accountable. Healthy teams will be talking openly about issues and resolving them.

Most attorneys don't want to meet with their employees this often, but for us, it's a proven process that has helped make our office a great place to work. When people come to work with a sense of purpose and mission, they do better work. When they feel heard, they are motivated to find solutions rather than complain about things they don't like.

HOW WE RUN OUR MEETINGS

Every meeting we hold has an agenda. We don't meet unless there is a clear purpose.

We always reserve the final minutes of any meeting to nail down what our next steps are and who will be responsible for taking them. These are often rocks or to-dos, but they can also encompass less crucial activities. Regardless of what it is, everyone in the meeting leaves knowing "who will do what by when"—a term many companies have given the acronym WWDWBW.

Successful meetings typically require advanced preparation. The most important one is making it clear to meeting participants what their role will be in the meeting. It might be as simple as saying on the meeting invitation that "everyone should come prepared to discuss our new paralegal training program." Or it could be more specific: "Kevin will walk us through the new features in our case management system."

We also try and make it clear how a decision is being made. Will it be an executive decision, or is the group deciding the matter democratically? This clarity can influence what and how much participants say, and it helps keep the conversation focused. A leader must clarify when she is soliciting input for her own consideration and when she is asking people to debate and reach a conclusion.

As the CEO of my firm, I have to remember to hold back my opinions until I've allowed others to speak. If I state my opinion at the beginning of a meeting, everyone tends to agree with me, killing the discussion and others' insight. It's not my job to walk into a meeting and show everyone how decisive I am. It's my job to flush out the facts and opinions and use those to reach the right decision.

Our best meetings have spirited disagreement. People argue their points with passion and respect, keeping personalities out of it. In the end, they agree to pursue whatever strategy the group settles on. Kim Scott, the author of *Radical Candor*, calls this "bumping up against each other." The process improves our work product and social skills.

I also try to be sensitive to everyone's personality preferences. Some of our team leaders are extroverted and outspoken. Others are introverted and like to think deeply before they speak. I consider it the leader's job to pull out the best ideas possible, and that means I have to coax certain people to speak. I don't give people the option to sit up against the wall and say nothing. That just means you're not putting in the same work that others are, and that's unacceptable. Everyone must contribute.

SUMMARY

Many of you reading this are probably thinking about how much you dislike meetings. You don't like attending them, and you don't like leading them. Consequently, many of you don't have meetings, or you have bad meetings.

I understand. I was once like you.

But I've seen the light, and all I can say is that you're missing a big opportunity to motivate your people and keep them all rowing in the same direction.

I was consulting with a large firm in the South recently, and we were discussing why it makes sense to file more lawsuits rather than settling quickly out of court. There are many reasons why this is a smart approach. Still, the firm's owners said they were certain that their staff attorneys would revolt and quit if they adopted a policy like that.

Would they? I asked.

Yes, one owner said. They don't want to change! They wouldn't understand why we'd want to do that.

"How often do you meet with your lawyers and discuss the firm?" I asked. "Not cases. The firm, and how it's managed."

"Rarely," the owner replied, "if ever."

So I described to the owner what a successful weekly meeting might look like. He could introduce the idea of filing more lawsuits and explain the data behind it. With this approach, his lawyers would make more money and have fewer cases. They would have more time to focus on the big, career-making cases all attorneys crave.

"You need to be the cheerleader and the teacher," I explained. "By the end of the meeting, your attorneys will be excited about this new change. Fewer cases. More money. Hmm. Why would anyone quit?"

The attorneys seated at the table glanced around at each other. Some arched their eyebrows. A few pursed their lips in thought. Fewer cases. Bigger settlements. You could hear the gears grinding.

"Well, let's get that weekly meeting started," the owner said.

THAT BIG CASE

As you can tell, we treat every case like it's that big, career-defining case that changes your life and your law firm forever. We don't wait around for a big case to walk through the door before we start working with urgency and attention to detail. We work that way every day.

But how do you ensure that people with those big cases come to you? How do you convince them to sign up with you?

We've cracked that code as well. Control your destiny and success by distinguishing yourself from the other lawyers in town. To do that, you have to understand your market and advertise wisely. In the next chapter, we'll explore what that looks like.

CHAPTER 5

CHERRY GARCIA
BEATS VANILLA

TO STAND OUT, YOUR ADS NEED A NEW FLAVOR

The scene opens with a friend and me walking toward a restaurant. It's a cold winter evening, and just as we reach the restaurant, I notice a guy climbing into his car. He drops his wallet. The guy drives off, so I grab the billfold and chase after him on foot.

A second later, an ambulance with its lights flashing passes me on the street. Now I'm running down the street behind the guy *and* the ambulance. People in the restaurant stop to stare. A waiter pulls out his cell phone and starts taking video.

Next thing you know, a television news station is airing footage of me running behind this ambulance. Suddenly, that clip is on several stations. Announcers in serious voices say, "Exclusive video of attorney Mike Morse *chasing an ambulance.*"

The shot moves to the inside of a living room where the TV news is on. The screen shows me running. The banner at the bottom says, "Mike Morse Ambulance Chaser?" As the camera shifts, you see my mom, Sue, in her stocking feet, watching this breaking news.

"Michael!" she says disapprovingly.

Then an analyst intones, "If you're going to hire an ambulance chaser, you might as well get one who can catch it."

The last shot is from the inside of a guy's car. He rolls down his window just as I run up, breathless.

"Hey, man," I say, holding up his billfold. "You dropped your wallet!"

To watch this commercial, go to YouTube.com/ mikemorselawfirm. Most of my commercials are there, along with my podcasts, interviews from television, and more. While you're there, subscribe!

The ambulance chaser commercial is just one of the dozens we've filmed in the last nine years that have made me and my mom household names in Detroit. I know when a commercial is a hit because I get hundreds of emails from strangers telling me how much they loved a particular commercial. Honestly, I can't walk down the street in my hometown without someone pointing at me or chuckling when they recognize me. They all yell out to me, "I love your commercials!" I always wonder if my competitors or other lawyers around the country get this type of positive, effusive response. My mom, a fixture in my commercials, is even more famous. People stop her and ask for an autograph or a selfie almost daily.

Not all my commercials are funny like this one. We made one with a client, Jesus, a triathlete who was severely injured when a bus struck him. Jesus recounts how the wheel of the bus crushed his right hand and his bike helmet, but he also describes how much triathlons and competition mean to him. While Jesus describes the accident, the footage shows him running and then slipping his right arm into a protective sleeve to train on his bike. As you are watching, you realize Jesus was able to come back from his devastating injuries. In the end, he not only competes again but takes second place in a race. And, in an emotional moment, he describes why he gave that medal to me in gratitude for handling his personal injury case.

"We shared bad times, so I wanted to share good times with him," Jesus says as the camera shows him hauling his bike out for an early morning workout. "You don't know what life will throw at you, or who will step in to save you." You can check this one out as well on our YouTube channel.

My commercials are different. Funny. Whimsical. Inspiring. They pack a punch, and they're memorable. They are a key reason our law firm has grown exponentially in the last decade. In January 2020, the National Trial Lawyers Association honored us for having the best thirty- and sixty-second legal ads in the country.

THE IMPETUS TO ADVERTISE

My firm got into TV advertising in 2011, the year Sid stopped sending us cases. We'd never advertised on television because one of Sid's rules was that if you took referrals from him, you couldn't run ads that competed with his on TV. With Sid gone, that restriction no longer applied to us.

But was TV the answer? Could television advertising make up for the loss of three-quarters of our cases? Would we get enough calls to keep all forty of our employees busy?

Twenty minutes after Sid fired us, John came back with an answer. We would continue to pay Sid his referral fees, of course. But if we took the same amount of money we were paying Sid and put this additional money into TV advertising, we could make up for all those lost Sid cases. Not only would we replace all those referrals, but we would also be signing up our own cases and keeping all the money we earned from them. TV advertising would generate enough cases that we could start referring out cases and using the referral fees we got to pay for future advertising.

It sort of made sense to me, but John was 100 percent convinced, so we moved forward. We had to get our name out and get the phones ringing, and television was the only way to do it. Social media marketing wasn't going to generate enough business. Billboards wouldn't do it. Radio might help a little, but we needed TV. The most prominent lawyers in Michigan get the core of their cases from TV advertising.

We budgeted a million dollars for the first year. The advertising budget came out of my pocket. It was a risk, but I was confident in my ability on television, and I knew we were the best law firm in town.

We never dreamed it would explode the way it did. We set a goal over five years ago to fund our advertising expenses through the referral fees we received, and I am happy to report that in 2020, it will. We refer out over a hundred new cases a week to about twenty different law firms—firms like mine was twenty years ago accepting cases from a big advertiser on television. These firms do a great job and appreciate the referrals. For us, our advertising is covered, and we aren't sending millions of dollars a year to Sid. However, we still take referrals from other firms who need our help.

To say it was a win-win all the way around is an understatement. Getting fired was the best thing that ever happened to us.

A NEW FLAVOR

At the time we decided to go on television, there were about ten attorneys in the Detroit area advertising on TV. Lawyers spent about $30 million a year in our designated marketing area. Sid was still one of them, and he was spending about $10 million a year. And he'd been doing it since the 1980s! How was I going to stand out in that crowded field? The public didn't know me. To make an impression, we had to spend heavily and make memorable commercials.

It helped that most of our competitors' commercials were bland. "We fight for you!" they said. Or, "We're the best." They hired low-wage actors to tell the audience, "These guys got me $10 million." I did my research and watched lots of lawyer commercials. I thought for the most part, they were all bad and the same. The public makes fun of them all the time. They were boring and tedious. I am not sure how this all started, but most lawyers just copy what the others are doing. They think it must work for him so it will work for me. They couldn't be more wrong. They all probably generate some calls, but it's not an effective model.

I couldn't stomach the idea of using the same approach. These commercials were vanilla flavored, and I was a Cherry Garcia guy. I loved the rich flavor, the tasty chunks of Cherry Garcia, and I wanted to create a message that was just as enticing. As we explored what that message should be, a key trait of our firm rose to the surface. Again, I thought back to our core traits of what makes us successful. We don't just fight hard. We aren't just good people and excellent lawyers.

We win.

Why had my firm grown so much? Because we won cases. I'd won ten trials in a row (most of which I shouldn't have won), so I had a knack for winning. We latched on to that as a central message. Mike wins. A friend of mine helped me secure a new phone number for the firm (855-MIKE-WINS), and our corporate email domain became @855mikewins.

The "Mike wins" message was based on gut instinct, but it was the right one. A few years ago, we did a brand study and learned that people looking for a personal injury attorney don't necessarily want an aggressive fighter on their side. What they want is someone who wins.

Mike wins. Call Mike.

COMFORTABLE IN FRONT OF A CAMERA

I also had confidence in my ability to sell. I'd been a good salesman from the time I was ten selling newspapers door to door. As a waiter for several years, I learned how to make people feel comfortable.

I'd also been on a couple of reality TV shows, and that taught me to be comfortable in front of cameras. I wasn't intimidated. I was telegenic.

We interviewed a handful of ad agencies, and we did several commercials that were different from the other attorneys'. We did some man-on-the-street-type interview commercials. They weren't bad, and they got the phones ringing.

Then in 2013, I met Ross Lerner from Lerner Advertising. He suggested a series of smart commercials portraying me as funny and a little self-deprecating. We brought my mom into the commercials and other family members as well. These commercials were unique and better than any others on TV at the time.

Most attorneys make cheap ads. The TV stations will often shoot ads for free. These ads are low quality, but many attorneys settle for them because they don't want to pay extra to shoot commercials. I made that mistake when I first started advertising, but I quickly realized I didn't like the lighting or sound quality. I wanted something better.

Ross advised us to make our new commercials with professional movie quality. The shoots went from being free to costing $20,000 and up. Instead of having a single camera operator and one person for lighting, our shoots with Ross had fifteen people, including an amazing director, Jeff Dougherty, multiple lighting people, sound technicians, makeup artists, and so on. It was like being on a movie set.

Our new approach blew away the market. The phone started ringing off the hook, and we started taking market share from other attorneys.

Many of our competitors responded by imitating our style. Their production values went up, and they started creating variations of my phone number or using the word WINNER in their ads. They started stealing my taglines and making fun of me in their ads. One guy started his commercial by saying, "We may not have the best hair in town, but..." Another had my image pop up with my firm name under it, asking questions such as, "Do you even know this guy?" It was desperate and funny at the same time. My competitors didn't like me busting into the market the way I did.

But it was too late for them, I'm afraid.

Despite the competition, we still dominate a competitive local TV market. We use data and focus groups to ensure we have the best commercials on the air. We've been on the Super Bowl six years in a row in our designated marketing area of Detroit.

We get hundreds of emails after a new commercial airs. We not only advertise our firm, but we also advertise our charity work. We advertise for the Humane Society. We advertise our public service. We're funny. We're serious. We're warm and grateful when the times call for it. We're brash. We make no bones about how we go after insurance companies on behalf of our clients. Ross came up with a tagline after one of our many brainstorming lunches. I was commenting on how much the insurance companies hate us, and he came up with, "No wonder insurance companies hate us. No wonder clients love us." We have been running that campaign to much success for many months now.

TV allowed us to scale massively. I went from being an unknown attorney in 2011 to being a household name in 2019. Annual settlements rose from $60 million in 2011 to $160 million in 2018.

TV fueled that trajectory, and with the business principles we adopted through Gino Wickman and John Nachazel, we were able to scale up and absorb that growth.

And that's a key point. You can have the best advertising, but if you don't have a handle on your numbers, hiring, goals, and growth, that advertising won't do you any good. As John likes to say, "You're only as strong as your weakest link." If you're planning to invest in TV advertising, make sure you have your business practices in place first to handle the resulting growth.

START SMALL BUT THINK BIG

We started by advertising on one or two stations. I wanted to break through the noise on a couple of stations rather than spreading our message too far and wide. As we saw results from the ads, we added a third station, and later we added a fourth and a fifth. We built up slowly.

Now we can afford to be on all the stations. Each station delivers a different type of client.

As our advertising budget grew, we moved outside of daytime television and sprinkled in some prime-time branding. Then we were presented with a last-minute opportunity to advertise on the Super Bowl. These local Super Bowl ads are not as expensive as the national Super Bowl ads but can still cost six figures for a thirty-second spot. However, those commercials reach millions of people who don't usually watch the daytime channels we advertised on, so we took the risk.

The results were spectacular. The Super Bowl ads dramatically raised my recognition level with the public. Now we shoot a special commercial for the Super Bowl each year. It's fun and creative.

In the first year we advertised on the Super Bowl, we calculated that we would need five incremental new clients to justify the expense of the costly ad. What we couldn't calculate was how long it would take to get those new clients. Well, it didn't take long. Within a day of the ad running, we'd signed up twenty new cases—four times what we needed to break even.

The Super Bowl ad is worth more to us than its cost. Our ad raises our stature in both the legal community and the community in general. Every judge, adjuster, facilitator, and defense attorney in our area sees it, and it helps us stand a little taller in their eyes.

We're respected. When we go into a case asking for a large settlement, people are more likely to take that offer seriously. When we tell a defense attorney, "We reject your shitty offer. We're happy to go to trial," they know we will. We haven't measured this effect with numbers, but we feel our advertising strengthens our negotiating position in all our cases. It elevates our game and gives our employees pride and confidence.

Our referrals from other attorneys and doctors also went up when we started advertising. Other attorneys refer to us because they know we'll follow through, and the client won't mind because the client is familiar with us and also holds our firm in high regard.

TV advertising enhances your integrity and reliability. These are the key by-products. Suddenly, you're a celebrity. People understand that you are highly skilled and wildly successful. They whisper your name when you walk into a room.

This side effect has helped us get calls, but it's also enabled us to serve people better. Clients are excited to meet me. They're respectful. They have a preconceived notion that I am trustworthy, caring, and professional. This helps me get what's best for the people we represent. In this sense, advertising has heightened the stature of our firm. It's strengthened our ability to advocate for our clients, and this allows us to get full value for them.

People often ask me, "How big do you need to be to consider advertising?"

There are two schools of thought.

One school says that you must spend as much as anyone of the top five spenders in your market. If you're not prepared to spend an amount equal to your competitors, then you should stay out of it altogether.

I don't see it this way.

In 2011, when I started, lawyers spent over $30 million on advertising in my market. Sid was spending around $10 million a year, and the rest were spending $2 million, $3 million, $4 million, or $5 million. I didn't have that kind of money to spend.

But I trusted my ability to compete, and I knew all these guys were older than me and had old and stale commercials. I was young, and I had a compelling pitch: I won.

I was lucky enough to have some money and was willing to bet on myself.

It doesn't matter whether your firm is just you, one partner, and one secretary. If you have confidence, creativity, and patience, and if you can tolerate the risk, you could try TV advertising. But your firm needs to have a functional business operation so it can handle the additional clients who come in.

Ross recently started working with an injury attorney in the Northeast. The attorney's commercials were decent, but he loved my ads and called Ross to help create something as good. They came up with some stellar ads. Ross has an uncanny ability to meet with someone and figure out the right value proposition for them.

After teaming up with Ross, this attorney's commercials changed dramatically. They portrayed the attorney as an everyday guy, someone who goes to bed early, returns books to the library, has a closet full of white shirts and gray suits, and mows his lawn to a precise height (measured by a ruler). He isn't the most exciting guy. He's pretty conservative and on the quieter side. You could call him a little boring. Ross used all of that to his advantage. He came up with some commercials that suggest that the greatest excitement in the attorney's life is when he hands his clients a big settlement check. Throughout the ad, the attorney comes across as funny, warm, hardworking, reassuring, and competent. He's a guy you can trust to help you out. From what I understand, the new spots are working wonderfully, and he is getting great feedback from the public.

LESSONS FROM TV

Here are a few more things we learned from TV advertising that might help others contemplating it:

◊ **Develop your theme, message, and personality.** What makes you stand out—are you better, faster, cheaper? We are the law firm that beats insurance companies and wins for our clients. We are funny and self-deprecating, but when it comes to our clients, we'll do anything to win. Even if you're not a client, if we find your wallet, we'll return it to you!

- **Most lawyers don't last a year on TV** because they can't stomach the investment. It's expensive, so if you're going in, make sure you have enough money for the long term.

- **Understand the difference between branding spots and call-to-action spots.** Both are critical to a successful marketing strategy. Using a good mix is vital.

- **It takes time for the phone to start ringing.** During the first months of an ad campaign, you are building awareness. You won't start signing up clients for a while. The first day one of our ads was scheduled to run—it was a Monday—I had ten extra phone lines installed so we could handle the influx of calls. I went to the switchboard that morning to watch the lights twinkling. Nothing. They didn't start ringing for weeks (but they haven't stopped since).

- **Advertising demands additional data.** It will take over a year to get a good, consistent volume of calls, and when those calls come in, it's wise to track them and correlate them to the advertising you're buying. What's the best geographic area to advertise in? What's the best time of day? What's the best station?

🔥 **Hire a leading agency.** We're still with Lerner Advertising. They collaborate with us on the content of our commercials, and it's a fun, creative process. We vet our plans through other sources, but the ad agency comes up with the majority of our TV commercial ideas.

🔥 **You have to be willing to spend enough to stand out.** If you don't do enough advertising, then what little you do will be a waste of money. You may not be able to spend what the top five marketers in your market are spending, but you must attract enough attention to make the spend worthwhile.

🔥 **Carefully research your market.** Here are the key questions to ask:

➜ Which law firms are already advertising in your TV market?

➜ How much are they spending?

➜ How successful are they?

➜ What are they doing with their cases?

→ What stations are they on?

→ What markets are they in?

◊ **Commit.** I get calls from attorneys in other markets wondering if they should advertise. If they don't have a decent budget, I tell them no. If they want to produce a simple, dull, vanilla commercial like their competitors, I tell them no. If they aren't willing to be vulnerable, show humor, or bring pets or family members into the commercial, I tell them no. But if they say yes to those questions, I introduce them to Ross Lerner. These attorneys can analyze the market and develop some new and interesting commercials and enjoy the success.

◊ **The more you spend, the more calls you get.** That may sound like the dumbest thing I can tell you, but it's the smartest. The more you spend, the more you make—provided the commercials are great. If you put garbage out there, you won't get the most lucrative cases.

◊ **Sometimes the most crowded market is the most lucrative.** In our market, the top nine marketers all spend the most money on Fox because it produces the best results. But to be effective in a jammed market requires that you put a concerted effort into standing out. You could be up against two other personal injury attorneys running commercials in the same two- or three-minute break, so you must ensure your commercials are better than theirs.

◊ **Get to know your market.** Almost every large market has four or five stations—ABC, NBC, CBS, FOX, and CW—and some stations reach different socioeconomic segments of the population. Imagine your ideal client and design ads for the stations that best reach that client. The programming is also crucial; is your ideal client watching soap operas, court TV, Jerry Springer, or *Green Acres*?

◊ **Hire an expert.** Although your local TV stations provide insight and your ad agency should have statistics on your market, we have an in-house media buyer who helps determine where our ads will have the most impact.

◊ **Use focus groups.** We show our ads and our competitors' ads to focus groups to learn how people react. Whom would they call and why? We've gleaned valuable insights from focus groups. Comments from a focus group inspired us to include my mom, Sue Morse, in our commercials. As I said before, our audience loves Sue and has made her a local celebrity. Including my mom in our spots was a game changer, or, as Ross Lerner would say, "a fastball waist high."

◊ **Be genuine.** Focus groups say I'm approachable and

likable. That's good to know because what you see of me on commercials is also what you get in real life. I'm not faking it in our commercials. I like to laugh and have fun, and it shows. If you don't have a great personality or you're boring or don't look great on TV, hire a spokesperson who has the qualities that reflect your firm.

◊ **Experiment.** If we're not sure whether we should advertise on college football games, we'll run tests to see what happens. What kind of calls did the ad generate? We also review our call data to determine the best times to advertise. We know calls drop off around Easter but when exactly? The Wednesday before or the Friday afternoon before? The answer will tell us when to lighten up our advertising and when to ramp up again. We found out, for instance, that we need to be on the Sunday evening news programs to get the phone ringing on Monday morning.

◊ **Track your calls.** When we first started, we tracked every single call to a specific commercial. We'd see that one type of ad generated sixty-four calls, but only one of those callers became a client. Meanwhile, a different type of ad—such as a client testimonial—generated eighty calls, and forty of them became clients. We could tell which new ads generated many calls and which older ads had lost their spark. This is harder to measure today; our clients have seen so many of our ads that it's hard for them to pinpoint the one that prompted them to pick up the phone.

◊ **Don't limit yourself to television.** Ninety percent of our ad budget once went to television, but it's 80 percent now because people watch more streaming content and record shows so they can fast-forward through the commercials. We've evolved with the times. We buy billboards and use Google Ads. We'll sponsor parts of news shows so that the crawler at the bottom of the screen will say, "This weather report brought to you by 855-MIKE-WINS."

A BIGGER STRATEGY

Although we've focused primarily on TV advertising in this chapter, television is just one element of a broader advertising strategy. We didn't advertise on TV when we were taking cases from Sid, but we were aggressive marketers in other areas.

Broadcast advertising by lawyers grew 70 percent between 2008 and 2015. Today, lawyers spend close to $1 billion annually. Many firms also spend heavily on paid search and social media efforts. The same states where broadcast advertising is most popular—including Texas, Alabama, California, Virginia, Nevada, and Wisconsin—are the same states with the most costly keywords related to legal matters.

In addition to television, we spend about $1 million each year on our digital campaigns. We use a firm (Caliber Legal, https://caliberlegal.com), and they do an amazing job for us, improving our website search engine optimization, pay-per-click ads, and ads on Facebook and Instagram.

PAID SEARCH

According to the Institute for Legal Reform, there are two ways lawyers drive search: by purchasing keywords from search engines to increase their ranking in search results, and by curating a suite of unbranded, informational sites that funnel traffic to the law firm's website.

Some firms are spending heavily on keywords. Search terms related to law firms, personal injury, and structured settlements are the most expensive terms on the internet. Twenty-three of the top twenty-five most costly Google keyword search terms are tied to legal issues. In 2015, some firms were paying over $600 every time someone clicks on their ad after a search for a term like "San Antonio car wreck attorney" or "accident attorney Riverside CA."

Meanwhile, firms are also assembling networks of informational websites that provide information to potential litigants while collecting their names and contact information. These sites often don't mention the law firm by name but allow it to rise to the top in nonpaid search results.

SOCIAL MEDIA

Some law firms also market their firms through social media, connecting to existing networks and tapping into conversations among key influencers, journalists, and advocates. The goal is to enhance a firm's credibility and name recognition. This type of "earned media" complements whatever broadcast, print, or search marketing the company is also doing.

This digital realm is the province of firms working on asbestos and mesothelioma. If you're working in that field, learn more about using social media to stay on top of it.

Law firms working in the area of data breach are also active on social media, conversing with journalists, publicizing class-action work, and, like the asbestos and mesothelioma folks, trying to build credibility.

OTHER STRATEGIES

Online marketing experts have a lot of other tricks up their sleeve that can help you appear in the search results when people are looking for a lawyer in your town. Here are a few tips:

🔥 **Make sure your website is mobile-friendly.** More than half of all searches originate from mobile devices, and users are five times more likely to abandon any site that is difficult to read on their phone. What's more, you must ensure your load time is quick; sluggish load times mean your bounce rate will be high as users leave your site without finding what they wanted.

- 🔥 **Use ad extensions.** Ad extensions are features that have additional website links, phone numbers, or locations. These can improve your click-through rate by up to 15 percent, and the longer ad you get shoves your competitors down the screen and hopefully out of sight.

- 🔥 **Cultivate more Google reviews.** Remember what we said earlier about the importance of reputation? It's vital, particularly in the legal profession, that people trust you. So make it part of your normal checklist to remind happy clients to post a review for you on Yelp, Avvo, Lawyers.com, or whatever site you want them to use.

- 🔥 **Get familiar with remarketing and Facebook retargeting.** This is when you're shopping online for something, and the website you're shopping on delivers a cookie. You're tagged with a code, and when you leave, either with or without purchasing something, the website can follow you around and drop ads in during your other internet stops. This helps you stay in front of your audience, and any clicks you get on those ads cost a fraction of a search engine keyword ad.

- ♨ **Consider a podcast.** My podcast is called *Open Mike*, and we launched in November 2019. In the first six months, we had almost 2 million downloads. Is it specifically making the phone ring with automobile and truck accidents? No. Is it keeping me relevant and attracting a new audience? Yes. Who knows what will come of it, but it is fun, and in these changing times, we are adapting and trying new things.

- ♨ **Radio and billboards.** Many firms have success with these two media outlets. According to the website InsideRadio.com, legal advertising on radio jumped 30 percent between 2015 and 2016, with over $100 million in sales. Although that's about a tenth of what lawyers spend on television, radio salespeople will tell you that their ads are a good complement to TV and digital ad campaigns.

- ♨ **Word of mouth.** Let's not forget that your happy clients are some of your best advertisers. Encourage your clients to mention you to their friends and business acquaintances, and make it a point of thanking them when they do. Direct mail advertising remains a valuable approach to finding new clients. Many marketing firms focus on direct mail advertising for lawyers, specializing in timing the campaign to find clients when they need you most.

SUMMARY

Our advertising budget has gone from $1 million a year to more than $8 million. I recently learned that I am twenty-ninth on the list of highest-spending attorneys in the country! The only limitation is our ability to attract, train, and retain people to handle the calls, get clients signed up, and work up the cases that result from advertising.

Some of you reading this book will never advertise on television—and for good reason. You might be a small firm that doesn't have the budget.

However, if you are a small firm interested in increasing your client base, consider some of the other options we've outlined here. The key is to zero in on your target audience and find a way to get in front of them when they need you.

If your firm has never advertised before but is interested in increasing revenue, start small. One of the best places to start is with digital advertising; according to several studies, the average person spends more time viewing digital media than traditional media.

Whatever type of media you choose—radio, television, digital, or direct mail—take the time to do it right. Be authentic. Be different. Be entertaining. Let your happy clients sing your praises. If potential clients don't know how great you are, they won't hire you.

CONCLUSION

HE WHO REPRESENTS HIMSELF
HAS A FOOL FOR A CLIENT

YOU DON'T HAVE TO GO IT ALONE

I hope this book has convinced you to adopt sound business practices for your law firm. We did, and it paid off.

It's made us 100 percent fireproof.

It's paid off for my firm, which has grown exponentially. We've learned how to hire, test, and organize our people in a way that makes them efficient, happy, and profoundly successful. Everyone embraces our core values. They are hardworking, loyal, dedicated to winning, and committed to providing outstanding customer service. They produce excellent work, and they have given my firm an excellent reputation.

I know this because we measure it.

Our transition from a hectic, unpredictable law firm to an efficient and proactive firm based on solid business principles has also paid off for me. Today, I work on only the cases I *want* to work on. I don't do any of the work I hate doing and don't do well. I have time for my family. I have time to eat with friends, colleagues, competitors, and clients. I have time to give speeches, do a podcast (openmikepodcast.com), travel, and write books. I have time to read and learn and grow.

I have endured significant setbacks—the loss of my father, the loss of my mentor, the loss of my office building to fire. My firm lost 70 percent of its cases *in one day*.

As I write this, the world is coping with the spread of the coronavirus. Some of my friends in the legal community have closed their buildings and laid off their office workers. They're scrambling to figure out how to keep the work flowing when their offices are shuttered and courts are closed. Millions of people have filed for unemployment in recent days, and no one knows how long this adversity will last.

But every day we remain sequestered in our homes, I'm

reminded how well-prepared my law firm was for this worldwide crisis. Because we are fireproof, we already had a disaster plan. All we had to do was take it off the shelf and follow it.

We closed on a Sunday, and the next day, all 150 of our employees were working remotely. Our employees had the right equipment, and it all worked because we had tested it beforehand. Everyone had the correct apps already loaded on their phones. People who needed printers got them, and those who needed any kind of office supplies got them delivered to their doorstep.

Not only did our plan work perfectly, but our people also stepped up. Several offered to take pay cuts. Many others asked to move to part time so they could care for young children or elderly parents. No one was interested in "stealing a paycheck" when they weren't working enough hours to justify their full salary. If they weren't able to give the firm their forty-hours-a-week attention, they didn't want a full week's pay.

That's what you get when you hire the best and treat them well.

We haven't had to lay off anyone yet. I am waiving my 2020 salary to help ensure we don't have to do that. I'm not interested in making panic-driven decisions to cut pay or lay off employees.

I don't have to panic.

I understand we may not hit our overarching goals this year. Our bonuses may not be as robust as in years past. But there is one thing I am certain will happen: we'll get through this.

My firm is fireproof.

UP AND RUNNING

If you think the practices we've outlined in this book will work for your firm, here are some tips for getting started:

- **Know your numbers.** The first step for any firm is to get a handle on your numbers. Sketch out a jumbotron (following the guidelines we lay out in chapter 3) and then pull your team together to discuss how to start collecting the numbers you need. The sooner you get started, the richer your database will be, and the more accurate your decisions will become.

- **Get the right people in the right seats.** Analyze your staff members and consider testing everyone to discover their true loves and strengths. Look for people who are clearly in the wrong seat and put them in a job that allows you to tap into their superpowers.

- **Establish your core values.** Ask yourself what your

firm does better than anyone else. Why do people come to you? What do they love about you? Who are the most productive and respected people in your office, and what are their core values? Most firms already have core values, but they've never formally identified them or demanded that every person in the company embody them. Core values make your decision-making easier. They help when you're hiring, and they keep everyone aligned and rowing in the same direction.

⚡ **Delegate and elevate.** If you're the firm's owner or CEO, perform the delegate-and-elevate exercise we describe in chapter 1. This exercise is crucial. The top person in your firm should be working on only things they love and are great at. They should delegate the rest to others (who can probably do a better job at those tasks anyway). Stop working *in* your business and begin working *on* it. When you're free of the drudgery, you can envision the future of the firm and where you want to take it.

⚡ **Find your integrator.** Every visionary needs someone who can make the dream a reality. I made my integrator my COO, but there are other ways to ensure your integrator has the authority to make decisions in support of the visionary's overarching goals.

⚡ **Don't be cheap.** Hiring a business coach will cost at

least $25,000 a year, and the best ones will charge more. Pay it. I had a friend here in Michigan, also a lawyer, who watched the success I had with Gino Wickman. So he bought Gino's books and tried to implement these changes himself. He had some success, but it was limited. So he hired an executive coach, and now his firm is growing. There is a direct correlation between how committed you are to the process and how much success you can achieve.

🔥 **Get the word out.** We talked about how we got into TV advertising and how it paid off for us. But I understand that not every attorney has the money or the desire to go on television. That's okay. You don't need to run ads on the Super Bowl. What you *do* need to do, however, is track where your cases come from. If it's all word of mouth, great. Find out who is talking and whether you can get them to do more of it. You've got to track what brings people to your firm so that if the numbers drop, you can adjust. Try different things. Try radio. Try billboards. Study the market. Know who the big advertisers are and where you're most likely to find your ideal customer. Whatever advertising you do, make sure it's high quality.

FIND A COACH

To enjoy the kind of growth my firm has, you'll need an

influential mentor or business coach. I was lucky enough to have two—Gino and my late father-in-law, Steve. I was fortunate because these advisors were persistent. I resisted their advice every step of the way and didn't act with commitment until I was at the end of my rope. Don't be as bullheaded as I was. Start now. I started in 2007, but I should have started much sooner.

This person doesn't have to be a lawyer, but they must be well versed in all of today's latest business practices.

Look for someone in your community who understands business the way you understand the law. While you were in law school, they were getting their MBAs. Look for someone who understands how to set goals and execute plans. These are crucial practices for any successful business, but they are probably foreign concepts to you. They didn't teach you these ideas in law school.

Lawyers can try to adopt these practices without any outside help, but the odds of you succeeding with that approach are slim. A coach who knows these principles can help you establish the groundwork for your newly structured law firm.

The right person becomes a driving force for your team, the kind of person you hate to disappoint. When I get close to one of our annual sessions with Gino, I set aside time to prepare. I make sure I've studied the right material and completed my rocks. I always feel like I don't have time for the meeting. Still, even after meeting five days a year for twelve years, I never leave a session with Gino without thinking, "Man, that was money well spent!" The sessions are always beneficial.

It's the best money I spend all year.

John feels the same way. When I mention the cost of a business coach, he points out that what we spend on mentoring has resulted in millions of dollars in revenue for our firm.

Not a bad investment, right?

If you find the right person, they'll know right away what a visionary is and what an integrator is. They'll help you find the right combination of the two. They'll know what core values are, how to identify them, and why they are essential to the culture of your firm. They'll understand how to evaluate and hire potential employees so that your teams are full of top talent.

They'll teach you how to set goals and keep your firm moving toward those goals with rocks, productive meetings, accountability, and jumbotrons. They'll help you start your jumbotron with the nine essential measurements. These metrics not only ensure your people are working at their best but will also enable you to forecast your firm's revenue and budget accurately. They will remove the guesswork. They'll help you not only *find* your sweet spot but also *stay* in your sweet spot so that you can have the most rewarding law career imaginable to you.

We hope this book and our website and materials will help you. We wrote *Fireproof* to convince you that this system works. We recommend that everyone in your firm—not just the lawyers—read this book and start adopting these principles. They are too important and too valuable to ignore.

NEW DOORS OPEN

The world might open up for you. It did for me. Free of the stress of uncertainty about my law firm, I could focus on other things.

When I started learning about the difficulties many kids in the Detroit school system have with getting the backpacks and supplies they need for school, I helped tackle that problem. We started small, buying 400 backpacks for one elementary school. The reaction from the students, teachers, and administration was amazing. The kids not only had a backpack stuffed with the best supplies; they now had self-esteem and a new regard for their education and their community.

So we did it again. Only the next time, we decided to give

backpacks to all 28,000 students in the Detroit Public School system. That was six years ago. We've done it every year since. That's 130,000 backpacks, and the number is growing every year.

Projects like this are just one of the rewards of running a sharp, business-minded law firm. So find that person who can help you the way Steve, Gino, John, and all the leaders and employees of my firm helped me.

Daniel Michel of the Arthur Law Firm in Defiance, Ohio, heard about our success and called for help in implementing our Fireproof process into his firm. Dan's firm has been a cornerstone of the small Defiance community for over fifty years. Still, the firm's attorneys had noticed a steady revenue decline in recent years. They decided to do something about it. We helped them refine their data, and I evaluated their current marketing practices. Now, Dan says, his office is planning for "a year of tremendous growth."

"Michael and his team offered us a solution that seemed too good to be true," Daniel says. "We had a chance to tap into the full resources of a top-flight plaintiff personal injury law firm, including the team that grew his law firm from $17 million in disbursements to over $160 million. It's been hard work, but our entire leadership team has embraced all facets of the Fireproof program. We are committed to the Fireproof method."

I know lawyers as well as anyone. I know what many of you are thinking right now. You're thinking, *This is too much. How will I find time to do my work?*

My response is: *you can.*

You must.

I understand your skepticism. I felt the same way. It took me years to accept these principles and find a way to implement them. But once I did, I felt like a fool for having resisted.

Here's the irony: If you decide you don't have time to adopt the practices we outline in this book, you are saying that you don't have the time to do the one thing that will give you more time.

Your life doesn't have to be that way.

We'll pull you along and help you become fireproof.

ACKNOWLEDGMENTS

This book would not be possible without the help, advice, and guidance of so many people along my journey. Many of these people are cited in the body of the book, but I want to take this chance to thank all my past and present employees. You are an inspiration to me.

Thank you to Amelia Anderson for suggesting I write this book and for always seeing more in me than I see in myself.

A special note of thanks to all the manuscript readers and others who made a direct contribution to the writing of this book. This list includes Keith Givens, Gino Wickman, Darren Findling, Jason Wagner, Justin Lee, Josh Linkner, Marc Mendelson, Damien Rocchi, Janet Rosenberg, and Melissa Nachazel.

Thank you to Joel Morse and Steve Radom for the lessons you taught me.

Thank you to my daughters, Jillian, Ella, and Lexie Morse, for being the reason I get out of bed in the morning.

Thank you to Harriet Morse, who was instrumental in the early days of my career and is a fabulous mother and a great friend.

Finally, I want to give a special thank-you to Jim Sloan, who brilliantly edited and assisted in so many ways in the creation of this book. I am proud of this book, and it is better because of your help.

ABOUT THE AUTHORS

MICHAEL J. MORSE is the CEO and founder of the Mike Morse Law Firm, the largest personal injury law firm in Michigan. He opened his office as a solo practitioner in 1995 and today employs 150 legal professionals.

Morse graduated from the University of Arizona with a bachelor of science degree in business with honors, and the University of Detroit School of Law, where he graduated cum laude with a juris doctor degree.

Morse lectures frequently throughout the United States. He also serves as a case evaluator and arbitrator in Wayne, Oakland, and Macomb Counties in Michigan. He is an executive board member of the Michigan Association for Justice and a member of the State Bar of Michigan and the American Association for Justice.

The Mike Morse Law Firm has received many awards, including *The Detroit Free Press* Top Place to Work award and *Crain's* Cool Places to Work in Tough Times award. In 2015, Morse received the Spirit of Detroit award for contributing backpacks and school supplies to 28,000 Detroit Public School students.

JOHN NACHAZEL is the chief operating officer of the Mike Morse Law Firm. A pioneer in the practice of applying business metrics to law firms, John's precise insights and financial forecasts have been instrumental to the firm's growth. John graduated from Miami University in Oxford, Ohio, with a bachelor of science degree in finance. He has an MBA from the University of Michigan in Ann Arbor and twenty years of sales and marketing experience.

CPSIA information can be obtained
at www.ICGtesting.com
Printed in the USA
LVHW111040210720
661194LV00008B/202/J